KINGDOM BUILDERS

KINGDOM BUILDERS

Witnessing, Dying, Moving

Dominic Smart

Authentic

First published 2005 by Authentic Media
9 Holdom Avenue, Bletchley, Milton Keynes, MK1 1QR, UK
and P.O. Box 1047, Waynesboro, GA 30830-2047
www.authenticmedia.co.uk

British Library Cataloguing in Publication Data
A catalogue record for this book is available
from the British Library

ISBN 1-85078-611-9

Cover design by Stephen Liddell
Print Management by Adare Carwin
Printed and Bound by J. H. Haynes & Co. Ltd., Sparkford

Contents

Acknowledgements

The questions and issues in this book were explored here at Gilcomston South Church in Aberdeen on Wednesday evenings through most of 2003, and at Hothorpe Hall in Leicestershire at the UCCF Staff-workers conference in January 2004. They came up again a couple of months later at Finlay Memorial Church in Glasgow, at their Missions weekend, and then in June 2004 at the Lakeland Bible School in Keswick. To the congregation here and to those involved in the other events I owe a huge debt of thanks for their perceptive and stimulating responses.

Similarly, Mark, Ali, Charlotte, Lucy and Jonathan at Authentic Media have patiently and encouragingly worked with me to bring the project to the point where you can hold this book in your hands. Its shortcomings are all mine.

Behind a book is an author, and behind this author stand a wife and four children who bear the greatest strains of a public ministry and yet by and large go unacknowledged. It is my privilege to have them recognised as far as this book will travel and by all who will read it. I love them dearly; to me, they are the most delightful and profound pleasure on this earth.

The aim of this venture is to help those who are called to be God's fellow-builders to glorify him. If the Father is pleased, if the honour of Jesus Christ increases and if the work of the Spirit is deepened, I will be a satisfied man. Who wouldn't be?

What This Book is About

So that you don't have to wade through pages of prose to get to the point, I have pulled the main bits into something that you can read while standing in a bookshop.

- This book is about the building of the kingdom of our God.
- It is about your place in that process, and God's work in you.
- It is a series of studies in the book of Acts which focus on the people involved in the building of the kingdom. It is not meant to be a commentary on Acts.
- It has the double aim of helping us to understand Acts as a story, and of helping us to recognise and respond to the work of God today.
- It approaches the book with one question that remains paramount throughout: *What did God have to do in these people's lives in order for them to become his fellow-builders?*
- A second question follows on: *What might God have to do to make me one of his fellow-builders?*

What This Book Is About

First Things First

The Book of Acts and the Building of God's Kingdom

On the face of it, tennis-coaching might not seem connected with either building or the book of Acts. But appearances can be deceptive.

How do we approach the book that comes between the gospels and the epistles? What does it teach us? In what sense is Acts useful for teaching, rebuking, correcting and training us in righteousness? How does the story of the growth of the kingdom of God equip the people of God for every good work? I'm taking it as a starting point that the book *is* useful: God says that it is in 2 Timothy 3:16, so it's up to us to discover, by the ministry of the church's great Teacher, the Holy Spirit, just how it is. These are crucial questions: the answers will help us to make sense of Acts and gain benefit from its amazing story.

How could we approach Acts?

A common way of approaching Acts is to regard it as laying down a pattern of good practice for evangelism and church planting. It gives us a picture of the means by which the church grew then and by which God will grow his church in our own days. Reading the book in this way, we are driven to the conclusion that the church grows by the spreading of the word of God through the preaching of the

1

gospel. In this way, the church of God grows numerically, in spiritual strength and in its geographical extent.

I find this approach to the book of Acts very helpful. It immediately opens up God's principles for his mission. It points me to the core task in a church-growing ministry; the preaching of the message of Jesus Christ in the power of the Spirit. It directs me to the content of the message, as I read just what those who spread the word of God actually said about him. It gives me an insight into the strategic nature of the growth of the kingdom of God: go for the major cities and towns in an area and then spread the gospel out into the surrounding area – preach it where the people are. It gives me a set of guidelines, a manual.

But there's a problem with taking *only* this approach to Acts. The book is not a manual.

Acts isn't written like a manual, doesn't read like one, and so shouldn't be used simply as if it were one. That's not to say that it doesn't do all the things that I just mentioned, nor that we shouldn't learn about the practical means by which the kingdom grows. But it does mean that we have to avoid plundering it for mission tactics alone. It is much, much more than a manual to teach us techniques for successful evangelism.

We run two dangers if we take only, or even mainly, that approach.

First, such plundering ignores the genre of the book: it's a story about people. These people are a new creation in Christ; they have the Spirit of God within them; they are under a commission that was not negotiated with them but simply given to them. They have a message to pass on, journeys to make, losses and pains to endure, faults to address, cultural baggage to lose, relational conflicts and theological differences to resolve. We read of them learning, travelling, fighting, suffering and dying, winning, changing and adapting, enduring and rejoicing. We see them in solitude, in company, in homes and councils, in deserts and cities. We read of conversations in palaces and prisons and of churches praying and sending. We see fallible and fickle humans being used by God to build a kingdom that will endure through all eternity.

Sounds familiar? Acts is a story; when we read it as a story, it immediately becomes more accessible to us. We can see ourselves more readily upon its pages. It therefore becomes more challenging than if we read it as simply a collection of practices for church leaders to copy. Those human elements challenge our deepest presuppositions about ourselves and some of our most cherished assumptions about church and ministry.

The second danger with the 'mere manual' approach is that we miss a vital theological aspect of the church's mission, be it in personal evangelism, church-based events or courses, church planting or overseas mission. Acts gives us a wonderful picture of the pastoral care that God shows for his fellow-builders. He is intensely interested in every aspect of their lives: he loves them – actively, intimately and strongly. The danger of taking only, or even predominantly, the instruction book approach is that God disappears from view. Instead of pointing us back to God, Acts then forces us back upon ourselves and our mission methods. The danger is that God's fellow-builders forget that the One who has called us is as concerned about the workers on the building site as he is about the building. After all, you are part of the kingdom that he has called you to build with him. His care for you – powerful and wise, personal and intimate – is central to what it means for him to be king. He is the *good* shepherd: the *good* king. The human dimension to Acts is essential because of what it tells us about God. Reduce Acts to a manual and you've reduced God.

Which brings us briefly to tennis-coaching.

Play Better Tennis ·

If you want to play tennis better than you do now (Mmm, maybe you don't play tennis, in which case just bear with me on this one) you'll go to a tennis coach. A good coach will, by and large, approach the improvement of your game in two ways. As you'd expect, they'll concentrate on your technique. They'll develop your grip to give you control of the racket head and to help you hit the ball hard without letting go – always an advantage in case you need the racket again. They'll work with you on your strokes, building up a repertoire, honing each one, training you to select the best shot automatically. They'll develop your tactical skills and expand your understanding of positioning on court. They'll train you to be deliberate about your footwork, balance, movement, weight distribution and the like. If they are worth the time and the money, they'll take your existing 'technique' apart and rebuild it piece by piece.

But they won't just concentrate on the techniques of play. They'll also, perhaps surprisingly for you, concentrate on the state of the player. They will work just as hard with you on the sort of a player that you need to be in order to learn and use the techniques effectively. So they will work with you on your fitness – your strength, suppleness and stamina. They'll spend hours working on your mental approach – your attitude, alertness, match-intelligence, competitiveness, ability to concentrate, and how to play 'in the zone', when the ball looks huge, seems to move slowly, and when the other side of the court seems to be one big gap into which you can fire any winner that you want. They will make you work on hitting the ball over the net, but they will also work on you.

Acts shows us the apostles and others in the infant church being used by God in the building of his kingdom. It shows us technique: method, ground strokes, footwork. But it is also a story of what God did in the lives of those through whom he was building his kingdom. It is the story of how God prepared, developed and fitted them to the task.

The Question

The approach to Acts that sees it as a manual asks the question 'What did these people do?' The approach that I'd prefer us to take in this book and its forthcoming sequel, is to ask 'What did *God* do in these people's lives for them to become his fellow-builders?' The answers to that question will have a profound effect on what we do, because they will affect who we are.

The follow-up question is the one that I hope will open us to the nature of our own calling: 'What might God have to do in *my* life?' It would be crass simply to use Acts to say that God will do everything in our lives that we see him doing with his co-workers in Acts. Yet the story of how God prepared and used his servants there does two things that help us to become more attentive learners. Firstly, it tells us what sort of God he is. He does this or that or the other kind of thing, so we should listen and worship accordingly. If we see God writing his own rule book, so to speak, then we listen and worship him as the all-wise, creative Sovereign, and in the service of his mission, we don't try and tell him that he can only do things our way. We get to know our God better. The stories in Scripture are as much a part of God's revelation of himself as the gospels or Romans or Revelation.

Secondly, it tells us what sort of people we might need to become. Acts tunes us onto God's wavelength a little more accurately so that we can anticipate the kind of things that we need to take on board in our own kingdom-building discipleship. God might do the kind of things in us that we see him doing here in Acts. We might not all have the kind of preaching challenges that Peter faced, for instance, yet we all use words to testify to the Saviour. So when we see Peter using words, we can learn. When we expect that there's something to learn, we become better listeners. How can my building work develop? What do we need to learn in our fellowships about the lives of God's fellow-builders?

One further point needs to be made very clear at the outset. The term 'fellow-builders' is awkward but maintains a vital perspective on who we are and what we are doing in life. We are only ever the builders of his kingdom as we take part in God's own building work. We are 'kingdom-builders' as the title of this book puts it, but not in the sense that we build God's kingdom for him, as if he had handed us a blueprint, a toolbox, a pile of bricks and a cement mixer and had then gone off to watch us from above. The Son ascended, but God sent his Spirit, who lives and works within and among us. God is no absentee boss, requiring occasional progress reports and making an annual visit. He is with us to make it possible for us to share in his work. We are kingdom-builders because he who is our life is building his kingdom. It's better for us to think of building with God, rather than building for God. That's true for four reasons.

The first is the obvious one: we can't! Once we were dead in our transgressions and sin but even now, made alive, we struggle with the problems caused by sin. We have learned much from this world that we have not yet unlearned but desperately need to. There is still so much of Christ's righteousness – all of which has been credited to us – that still needs to be woven into our lives. We are still eminently prone to spiritual seductions. We simply cannot build God's kingdom for him.

Secondly, it is *his* work. The mission of the church is the mission of God. He promised that the serpent's head would be bruised (Gen. 3:15). He said that he would bless all nations through Abraham's seed (Gen. 22:18). The Scriptures teach that 'unless the Lord builds the house, they labour in vain that build it' (Ps. 127:1). His zeal would accomplish the ever-increasing government of his anointed one (Is. 9:7). Jesus said, 'I will build my church and the gates of Hades will not overcome it' (Mt. 16:18). His is the motivation behind all mission; his is the wisdom by which it is planned; his is the power by which it is accomplished; his is the grace with which the kingdom is built. It is his mission that we are to be brought in on, not our mission that God has to be reminded of whenever we turn to him for a bit of extra help.

Thirdly, we are *fellow*-builders because of what defines us as Christians. Our life is life in Christ. Not in any way do we have one ounce of life – righteous and eternal life – outside of Christ. When, in John 15:5, Jesus said 'Apart from me you can do nothing' he wasn't simply stating that we need his help. He was crystallising into one statement of fact all that the imagery of the vine and branches was teaching: we need his *life*. Grafted into Christ, 'our' sap and fruitfulness are actually his life in us and his fruitfulness through us. Because he is the true vine, we can be fruitful only as branches grafted into the true vine. He is the one true kingdom-builder. But here is the staggering thing: we are made to be his fellow-builders by virtue of our union with him. Have another look at Psalm 127:1. It does not say that because he builds there will be *no* labourers. It says that because he is building, our work is rescued from its futility. It is both a

caution against seizing control of the building job, and a
promise of productive building when we relinquish
control. It's a mercifully clear warning against grinding
ourselves into the dust out of sinful self-trust, and a
promise of genuine success when we join in with his
building work. That's one of the wonders of his grace: he
makes something of our lives. We are lifted from the
world's fading glory to the plane of God's eternal glory
and from the plane of this world's futility to the plane of
his eternal effectiveness. Because we are in him, our lives
– every bit of them, not just the religious bits – are given a
significance that far outweighs any mundane notions of
importance. Even when the Bible talks about our labour,
our costly toil, being not in vain but of eternal value, it's
not our labour *for* the Lord that is referred to, but our
labour *in* the Lord (1 Cor. 15:58).

He is on a mission to build his kingdom; you are in
him; so you are his fellow-builder.

Fourthly, the Bible itself describes us as participants in
the work of God. Three times Paul speaks of himself and
his companions in mission as 'God's fellow-worker(s)':
'For we are God's fellow-workers; you are God's field,
God's building' (1 Cor. 3:9); 'As God's fellow-workers we
urge you not to receive God's grace in vain' (2 Cor. 6:1);
'We sent Timothy, who is our brother and God's fellow-
worker in spreading the gospel of Christ' (1 Thes. 3:2).

What a relief to be God's *fellow*-builders! It takes so
much of the strain out of service. It also opens up a vast
new area of 'skills' for us to learn: chiefly to do with
listening and discerning what God is actually doing
wherever he has placed us, in the lives of those around
us. It opens up new possibilities, for with God nothing is
impossible. It opens up new hope: no longer are we
consigned to the dust heap of unloved Christian failures,
for we have always been failures with God yet he loved

us and gave his Son for us when we were sinners. We can, in Dietrich Bonhoeffer's words, dare to be sinners: we can dare to admit to weakness and inability. It opens up new faith: for now we are not stuck with trusting ourselves and our methods but are directed to trust and rest in the One who will accomplish his purpose. It opens up new joy: joy that is freed from self-congratulation and can take real delight in the work because of the True Worker who is delighted to have us work with him. It opens the way to new praise, for we were made to glorify him, not the church nor ourselves. As the kingdom is built, the glory goes to God; and, paradoxically, that's much more deeply satisfying for us.

What is the Kingdom of God?

There's one remaining point to make clear before we dive into Acts and the work of God in his fellow-builders. It's about the nature of God's kingdom. Just what exactly *is* it that he's called us to build with him?

Our natural tendency, when we hear of a kingdom, is to think about a place. When we read the parables of the kingdom in the gospels we read, occasionally, of something that's like a place – you can enter it or not, there's a gate across the entrance, etc. But the geographical images are just that – imagery. The best way to get to the heart of the teaching about the kingdom of God is not to think about a place but to think of the ordering of life under a king. Think of the rule of the heavenly king, the Anointed One, the Messiah, Jesus the Christ. Don't think geography, think sovereignty. Don't think king*dom*, think king*ship*. The question that the kingdom of God forces upon everyone who hears about it is not 'What's your address?' but 'What's your relationship to the king?' The kingdom of God is wherever his kingship is acknowl-edged. Clearly he is king *de facto*, whether or not anyone acknowledges him as being so – hence the kingdom is both here and not yet here. It is where he is worshipped and obeyed that we find the kingdom. It is, at its heart, not merely kingship *per se*, but kingship that people have seen and to which people have yielded. It is a matter of how we relate to the king: is it self-ruling rebellion or is it loyal submission, faithful service, and the homage of worship? Are you under the gracious rule of his lordship or under your own rule – which is really the tyrannical rule of the prince of darkness? And are you under the protective power of the king's mercy or are you to be judged under his awful wrath?

Among other things, this means that the day will come when the kingdom reaches its full extent as every knee bows and every tongue confesses that Jesus Christ is Lord. The day will come, as John saw it in Revelation 11:15, when every rebellious refusal of him in this world will end and the 'kingdom of this world' will 'become the kingdom of our Lord and of his Christ'.

For this reason alone it should be the aim and the delight of every Christian to see the king thus honoured. To be made God's fellow-builders is to be made into what we should want to be more than anything else.

Chapter 1

Peter: Healer and Preacher

Have you ever wondered how we can be like Jesus in terms of mission? We're familiar with the need to be like him in our character and behaviour, but reflecting the One to whom we look also carries over into our impact upon this world – that is, into our mission. A foundational principle of the Christian life is demonstrated to us over and over again in Acts: *being fellow-builders, we do what the true Kingdom-Builder does.* It's not surprising when you think about it: we have Jesus' life, we have his righteous relationship with the Father, and we have the Spirit of sonship within us so that we cry out 'Abba, Father.' We love the same things, share the same values, long for the same glory, and one day will be at home in the same house. When we are engaged as his fellow-builders, we find ourselves doing the same kind of thing as him in the same kind of way and with the same kind of results. So we become like him in our character, conduct and mission. That's the wonder, the fantastic privilege of having Jesus as the 'Proper Man', as Martin Luther called Jesus – the 'second Adam' that Paul describes in Romans 5. As well as being our life, he is also our pattern, the One we grow up into so that we find ourselves called to serve as our Saviour, the 'Proper Servant' served.

It's in Acts 3 that we begin to see this pattern and principle functioning. We see it at the gate called Beautiful, and a beautiful thing it is. Watch for this as the scene unfolds: we, worked within by God, work the works of God.

The scene

As was their habit, Peter and John go up to Herod's magnificent edifice, the Temple of Jerusalem, to pray. They are still worshipping God there, bringing the worship that belongs to the new covenant into the structures of the old covenant. As they go in, they meet a man who is lying on the ground by the Gate Beautiful. He has been crippled all his life, so he is entirely dependent on other people to move him around (notice that he's been carried there). He has to beg: that's his only way of gaining income. Giving to the poor was a good thing to do: together with fasting and prayer it was one of the three pillars of Jewish piety. So it was entirely in order for him to be there at the Temple; the practice of begging wasn't seen as the social disgrace or civic embarrassment that it is nowadays; at least, not by those who didn't need to do it. Crowds of people passed him who would count it a blessing to be able to throw some loose change in the direction of the poor. Get the almsgiving done and you could enter the Temple and pray successfully, even more so if you'd also skipped breakfast and lunch!

Peter the healer

It is into this situation that Peter and John enter. No one else would have bothered to look at the man; they would have had no interest in him as a human being. People simply threw money in a heap on the floor. If we read the passage carefully we can work out that the man's head was down; he wasn't looking at who was going past. For him, the shame of begging, plus the discomfort of having to look up at people who would have the bright sky behind them, meant that he would simply be watching feet go past, calling out for money, and waiting for the chink of coins as they landed in his bowl. Anonymous feet, anonymous cash, no humanity.

But Peter and John stop. They look straight at him and speak to him: they invite him to look at them. Suddenly, in the midst of impersonal and routine religious practice, a personal encounter is happening. It isn't just charity that is being doled out. There is something about Peter and John which engages with people; which creates this kind of gospel encounter. To everybody else going in this man is just an object, but not to these reborn, Spirit-filled men. The Holy Spirit's work in them has turned them into people who have to engage as fellow-human beings with those in need.

Notice Peter's priorities. He could rush on in. It is about the time for prayer – 3 o'clock in the afternoon so there's not really much time for dilly-dallying. Yet their priorities are not dictated by the clock (or by the sun dial!).

He could give priority to the silver and gold. Peter and John could go away and put a little contribution together. It is, after all, what the man is asking for; and believers are selling their possessions and goods and giving their money to anyone who has need (Acts 2:45). So they could dip into the benevolent fund and take it back to the Gate Beautiful. But they don't. They have different priorities. Peter has something better, which the man needs more than silver and gold. Peter has something that nobody else going into the Temple can give to the man; something which, silver and gold could not buy. He has Christ and all his blessings to give.

So Peter passes on his prize possession. He is not smug because he's sorted; the blessings that he has received were not given to him for him alone. Peter was remade and filled with the Spirit to be a witness, to pass on what he knows and has. He is not a bucket: he is a channel. Peter gives the most valuable thing that he has ... 'Silver and gold I do not have, but what I have I give you.'

He does this with power and authority. 'In the name of Jesus Christ of Nazareth, walk!' He doesn't suggest it, or offer it as an option. It comes as a command – walk! Notice how he phrases it. 'In the name', that is, by the power and authority of Jesus Christ. But look even more closely at what he says: 'In the name of Jesus Christ of Nazareth.' This is still close to the crucifixion, and to the testimony given on the day of Pentecost. That phrase 'Jesus Christ of Nazareth' is a hot phrase in Jerusalem. It's not just 'Jesus'– there were hundreds of Jesuses around. It was a very popular name. Recall the inscription that was nailed above Jesus' head: INRI – Jesus of Nazareth, king of the Jews. Jesus Christ of Nazareth is the buzz phrase for the One who was on that cross on Golgotha. By *this* Jesus, who is most famous in Jerusalem for having been crucified and then reported as having been raised from the dead, in the name of *this* Jesus, walk! (He is going to develop precisely this when he preaches in a few moments.) Peter has no power or authority of his own. Neither does John. None of the apostles have. They do it all in the name of Jesus Christ of Nazareth.

And Peter gives practical help. 'Taking him by the right hand, he helped him up' (3:7). He didn't just give the command and then stand back and watch. He helped the man up. It's thoughtful and kind. The man had never walked before, never even stood on his own two feet before. He would have needed a hand up.

The cripple walks, leaps and praises God. In public, which is significant. The healing has been done in Jesus' name: Jesus is being publicly honoured. He had been humiliated and rejected publicly on the cross. Now he is being honoured publicly by this miracle done in his name. But there's more. The impact of the resurrection is being made public: his kingdom didn't die with him. In his ministry, his miracles were, among other things, signs of his kingship – they declared that he was the Messiah, to be acknowledged and received joyfully as such, or to be rejected as such. The continuing of those messianic signs declares not only that the king is alive again, but also that his kingdom is going to thrive even more, proliferating and progressing through the world that had thought to put him to death for precisely his claim to be king.

Peter the Preacher

Seizing the moment

Peter has become a healer. He couldn't do that in his own power or authority; but he had become a healer in Jesus' name. He hadn't been much of a preacher before Pentecost either, but the Spirit has changed that as well. We're about to see that change have its impact again.

The healing causes quite a stir. The man is still holding onto Peter and John. They have helped him up and he doesn't let go. So he walks with them into the Temple courts, leaping and praising God and clutching Peter and John. They thought they were going in for the usual sedate prayer meeting but it turned out quite differently. Peter finds himself surrounded by people who, recognising the man, are astonished at what's happening. They run up to Peter, John and the man in the place called Solomon's Colonnade.

What does Peter do? He could run as well – for cover!
The crowd could have been embarrassing but it also
could have been intimidating. He is in the Temple now,
on the Sanhedrin's turf. He's going to be put on the spot.

But he does not run. He seizes the moment. For you and
me, 'seizing the moment' might well *not* mean that we speak
to huge crowds as Peter was doing here. But will mean that
we respond to those whom God brings to us. Peter and John
responded to the man, crippled, by the gate. Now Peter will
respond to the crowd. Better, Peter responds to the situation
that God has set up for the sake of the gospel: it's as much
responsiveness to God's moment as it is to the people, even
though they are more visible to the human eye.

Seize the moment for the gospel. Whatever it is and
however small that moment might seem, however
unexpected, however inconvenient, seize it.

Our natural response is often to let go of that moment
as quickly as possible. Something in us, rightly, does not
want to draw attention to ourselves. We feel that being a
witness has nothing to do with our own prominence or
our egos. But Peter doesn't seize the moment for himself.
Remember that Peter is the one who denied Christ. This
is Peter the scaredy-cat. Peter wasn't used to seizing
moments like this. But he will seize the moment for Jesus
Christ and the gospel. This is God's moment here and
Peter cannot let it go.

We're not going to go through all the details of what he
says in this open-air, evangelistic sermon. But I do want
to take account of some of the points that he presses on
the hearers as he preaches Christ.

He is your God's glorified servant

By saying 'The God of Abraham, Isaac and Jacob, the God
of our fathers, has glorified his servant' (3:13) he is

hooking right into where they were most sensitive. We need to find that line into where people are, to what is important in somebody's world. Peter found it immediately because, like them, he was going in to pray to the God of Abraham, Isaac and Jacob. *Our* God has glorified his Servant.

For the devout Jews who were going up to the Temple to pray, their family trees, which they could trace back to the Patriarchs, were among their greatest signs of honour. Now, Peter says, this God, to whom you were about to pray and into whose good books you sought to earn a place by giving alms, *this* God whom you claim as yours is the very One who has glorified his Servant, in whose name this healing was done. The four 'Servant songs' in Isaiah, in chapters 42, 49, 50, and 52 to 53, are behind what he is saying here. The Servant is both appointed by God to his task and anointed by God for it. By being faithful to God he will bring justice and peace, proclaim good news to the poor, suffer death as the Saviour and sin-bearer, be glorified after suffering, and prolong his days beyond death. Inspired! It puts them in an awkward position, doesn't it? They're not talking of something done in the name of a foreign god. This is their God who has been at work. And their God has honoured the One whom they have crucified.

You killed the wrong man!

Which leads him to the cross and the resurrection. He is incredibly blunt when he says 'You killed the wrong man!' Of all the people to put on the cross, this was the wrong one. You disowned the One who has made you for himself and who made himself yours. You disowned the holy and righteous One in favour of a murderer. What an incredible irony! You asked that a murderer be released to you. That's the kind of people you are. You'd rather have a murderer let off. You feel more affinity for a murderer than you do for your covenant God.

Repent ...

He presses the point home to the crowd with the most devastatingly ironic sentence in the whole of the preaching of the gospel in the New Testament: 'You killed the author of life.' 'You killed' ... Don't blame the Romans, don't blame the Sanhedrin. You were there. You shouted 'Crucify him!' You bayed for his blood. But God vindicated the One whom you killed. God raised him from the dead and we are witnesses. As you saw this man being healed, so we saw Jesus raised.

Peter makes their offence as clear as can be. He lays their accountability before *their* God right at their door. So what are they going to do? The right response was just the same as it had been on the day of Pentecost. When the people had heard the gospel then and said to Peter and the other apostles, 'Brothers, what shall we do?', Peter had replied, 'Repent and be baptised, every one of you, in the name of Jesus Christ for the forgiveness of your sins.' The response was still the same. You must repent.

'Repent, then, and turn to God' (verse 19) for there are many blessings found by that route that can be found by no other. Repent 'so that your sins may be wiped out' (first blessing). Repent 'so that times of refreshing may come from the Lord' on you and on Israel (second blessing). And repent 'that he may send the Christ', in all his glory, the great king over all the earth who has been appointed for your restoration as the people of God (third blessing).

The Emerging Pattern

We, worked within, work the works of God

As I suggested earlier, a principle echoes through the
lives of Peter, Stephen, Philip and Paul. It will echo
through all God's fellow-builders, you and me included.
We, worked within, work the works of God. Jesus said
that the Spirit would come and bring to them the things
concerning him. The Spirit would be another 'helper',
that is, another of the same as Jesus. With the Spirit, the
apostles would do even more wonderful things than
Jesus had done, because they're going to be able to do
them all over the world. Jesus healed – Peter heals. When
Jesus healed it was a sign of a kingdom coming, a king in
their midst. Would those who saw the healing believe the
king or would they reject him? When Peter heals, it's a
sign that the kingdom has come right there in Jerusalem
in their midst. Though they tried to destroy the king, God
raised his Anointed One from the dead and the kingdom
is still at work and advancing. Jesus healed almost at the
start of his ministry. Peter is healing almost at the start of
his ministry. Jesus preached to those who saw his
miraculous healings – Peter preaches to the crowd who
came because of the healing. Jesus preached repentance.
Peter preaches repentance. You see what is happening?
Peter, worked upon and within by the Spirit, works those
works that the Father did through Jesus Christ.

That principle is going to work through the other lives
that we will look at in Acts. It works in our lives also. We,
worked within, work the works of God. If we want to live
the Christian life we are going to live a different life from
everybody else around us. We won't be able just to merge
in. We will look at people differently. We will assess their
needs differently. We will have different priorities in our

own encounters with people. We will pass on our most prized possession. We will work with power and authority that come from God and not from us. We will work, live and serve, speak and bear witness in the name of Jesus Christ of Nazareth. We will reach out and help people. The life of the disciple is patterned on the Master, so we should expect to see his pattern in our lives. When we encounter people in the supermarket, or at the bus stop, or sitting next to them in lectures, or working with them on a project, or wherever it happens to be, we, worked within, will work the works of God. By that means God's kingdom will extend. It's not going to happen by me and you wanting to be like everybody else and fading into the background. It happens by God working within us, so that we work those works by which the kingdom will be built.

To ponder

Think of your different spheres of activity – perhaps your work or your studies, your family or church, your neighbours or the people with whom you pursue a sport or hobby:

- In what ways can you set up signs of the presence of the king?
- How might you point to his compassion or his truthfulness, his righteousness or grace, his wisdom or justice? How might you work the works of God?
- Think specifically for whom you can set up these pointers – names would help here.
- Pray now for God to set up the moments and for the discernment to spot them; for the courage and love to seize the moments.
- What do you usually see as the needs of people in these different spheres of life?

- Are there aspects of your background, education and social grouping that blind you to the poor, the socially disadvantaged, the despised? Are there aspects of the life of your fellowship which do the same?
- Next time you go shopping, notice people. The girl on the check-out, the shop assistant to whom you speak, the person who serves you coffee – do they register as real human beings, or are they insignificant? Do you avoid eye contact? Do you speak to them or do you tend to grunt and move off? Do you smile at them? Do you dump your bad moods, impatience or irritability on them?

Chapter 2

Peter and the Crunch

Is there such a thing as cost-free Christianity?

In the sense that we are saved by the free grace of God, yes. We cannot negotiate our pardon. We pay no ransom. Were mercy for sale, it would not be mercy. If grace had a price, it wouldn't be grace. We cannot buy his love: love is not a commodity, God is not a trader and heaven is not a market.

That said, your Christianity will cost you everything. The true Builder of the house of God hadn't a home to call his own and was despised and rejected by those he came to save. It was not through earthly success but through suffering that Jesus became the perfect representative of humanity and the perfect substitute for those with broken lives. He asked those who followed him to take up their cross – every single day of their lives. Your Christianity can never be cost-free in terms of discipleship.

Throughout Acts, it cost God's fellow-builders their comfort and convenience. Some of these new Christians would lay down their lives. The troubles that hit them were never a mark of them having gone off the rails. Quite the opposite: they were always a sign that they were still firmly on the same track as Christ. Neither was the price somehow the downside of the privilege of being a fellow-builder of an eternal kingdom, as if the building was the silver lining and suffering the cloud. The cost was the privilege; suffering with Christ was the silver lining.

Peter has to start paying the price of responsive and loving obedience. There was the miracle. (Great! Signs, wonders, God at work; the breakthrough has come, hallelujah!) There was the gospel preaching. (Marvellous preaching of the word – clear and faithful in its content, challenging in its impact; just the thing that the church needs more of.) Now there is a price to pay. (What?!)

The priests and the captain of the temple guard and the Sadducees came up to Peter and John while they were speaking to the people. They were greatly disturbed because the apostles were teaching the people and proclaiming in Jesus the resurrection of the dead. They seized Peter and John, and because it was evening, they put them in jail until the next day. But many who heard the message believed, and the number of men grew to about five thousand. The next day the rulers, elders and teachers of the law met in Jerusalem. Annas the high priest was there, and so were Caiaphas, John, Alexander and the other men of the high priest's family. They had Peter and John brought before them and began to question them: 'By what power or what name did you do this?' Then Peter, filled with the Holy Spirit, said to them: 'Rulers and elders of the people! If we are being called to account today for an act of kindness shown to a cripple and are asked how he was healed, then know this, you and all the people of Israel: It is by the name of Jesus Christ of Nazareth, whom you crucified but whom God raised from the dead, that this man stands before you healed. He is "the stone you

builders rejected, which has become the capstone."
Salvation is found in no-one else, for there is no other name
under heaven given to men by which we must be saved.'
When they saw the courage of Peter and John and realised
that they were unschooled, ordinary men, they were
astonished and they took note that these men had been
with Jesus. But since they could see the man who had been
healed standing there with them, there was nothing they
could say. So they ordered them to withdraw from the
Sanhedrin and then conferred together. 'What are we
going to do with these men?' they asked. 'Everybody
living in Jerusalem knows they have done an outstanding
miracle, and we cannot deny it. But to stop this thing from
spreading any further among the people, we must warn
these men to speak no longer to anyone in this name.' Then
they called them in again and commanded them not to
speak or teach at all in the name of Jesus. But Peter and
John replied, 'Judge for yourselves whether it is right in
God's sight to obey you rather than God. For we cannot
help speaking about what we have seen and heard.' After
further threats they let them go. They could not decide
how to punish them, because all the people were praising
God for what had happened. For the man who was
miraculously healed was over forty years old (Acts 4:1–22).

Surprise, Surprise!

A miracle, followed by teaching, with a price to pay.
Where else do we come across that in the Bible? Peter,
having been with Christ and now full of the Holy Spirit,
begins to go over the familiar course of Jesus' own
ministry. Within Peter's life, the life of Jesus is re-
patterned. For Jesus, healing miracles were followed by
teaching and the teaching drew hostility. Opposition

arose from the Jewish authorities because of the teaching with which Jesus seized the moment, pressing home the implications of the miracle. The experience of the church in the book of Acts is the experience of those who have received the Spirit of Christ. He descended on the believers at Pentecost and repeatedly fills them for their work throughout the rest of the book. It's no surprise that since Christ faced opposition, Peter, filled with the Spirit, also faces opposition. It certainly would have come as no surprise at all to Peter: Jesus said that this is what would happen. Jesus spelled .out that the connection between the course of his life and the life of his disciples would mean opposition and persecution.

If the world hates you, keep in mind that it hated me first. If you belonged to the world, it would love you as its own. As it is, you do not belong to the world, but I have chosen you out of the world. That is why the world hates you. Remember the words I spoke to you: 'No servant is greater than his master.' If they persecuted me, they will persecute you also. If they obeyed my teaching, they will obey yours also. They will treat you this way because of my name, for they do not know the One who sent me. If I had not come and spoken to them, they would not be guilty of sin. Now, however, they have no excuse for their sin. He who hates me hates my Father as well. If I had not done among them what no-one else did, they would not be guilty of sin. But now they have seen these miracles, and yet they have hated both me and my Father. But this is to fulfil what is written in their Law: 'They hated me without reason' (Jn.15:18–25).

Perhaps verse 19 is one of the best examples we have of what the Bible often means by 'world'. Here and elsewhere, it doesn't primarily refer to things geographical.

'The world' is not 'all the countries of the world' or 'the whole planet'. Clearly it can't mean that, or else when Jesus spoke of us not being in this world and being chosen 'out of it', he would have been talking about some kind of interstellar transportation! ('Beam me up Lord!' – it's tempting to want it, but it's not what God has in mind for us, not yet anyway.) It's not so much a place as a way of organising life: it's a system. In the New Testament, it's a way of ordering life in rebellion against God, even if the rebellion takes a religious form. 'World' is life ordered under its own authority. As the saying goes, it's not the world in its bigness; it is the world in its badness.

It is the magnificence of grace to save rebelliously organised people from the consequences of their 'world-ish', deathly existence and give them eternal life. The world being what it is, all that God does for us he does by grace. By definition, 'the world' is opposed to the kingship of Christ. Do we anticipate opposition to the growth of the kingdom? If not, we've neither understood the kingdom nor the world. But don't lose heart, for we are not to expect *only* opposition. Remember the purpose and the power of God!

Was this just for those disciples then? No. Was Jesus speaking about rare and exceptional circumstances that might arise for a few in the life of the church between his first and second advent? I don't think so. In John 15 he is making a point for the benefit of all his followers so that they might understand rather than misread what happens to them. He wants them to know what a normal life will be like for them – the norms being those that apply in his kingdom, not the normal life according to the way the world thinks. 'If they persecuted me, they will persecute you also.' Did they persecute him? Yes. Then, if we live as those who are taken out of the 'world' by Christ, chosen out of the world by Christ to live under *his* sovereignty and his Messiahship, as night follows day, opposition will follow kingdom-building ministry.

Jesus paints the pattern so clearly for us. 'I spoke, the world hated it and persecuted me. I did kingdom deeds and when the world saw them for what they were, it hated me. Since the world hates me from the heart, the world persecutes me. When you do these things, the "world" will do that to you as well.'

We don't want a persecution complex; neither do we want to invite opposition so that we can feel perversely good about ourselves. But if we're having a really easy time of it in this world and it's costing us nothing to follow Jesus, then we have to ask ourselves, 'Am I really following *him*? Or have I confined him to a corner of my life where he can be harmless, comforting, controlled? Am I actually taking up my cross as he took up his?' If it's costing me nothing, am I really following him or have I worked it so that really I've got him following me? The way Jesus speaks to the disciples, paying a price is the norm. Kingdom-building brings hatred and opposition. It's no surprise.

The Opposition

It's quite a syndicate. The priest, the captain and the guards have responsibility for good order in the Temple. They ensure right and proper observation of ceremonial worship: sacrifices, prayers, almsgiving. They keep Gentiles and women out of the areas that they are not supposed to enter. They make sure that Jewish men only go into their allowed areas at the right time and in the right way. They also see to it that nobody, but nobody, goes into the place that nobody but the High Priest should go to. They have religious backing from the Pharisees, and they have political allies who safeguard their power and authority: these allies are found in the party of the Sadducees.

They are deeply disturbed simply because the two apostles are actually teaching, which unauthorised people weren't supposed to do. The apostles aren't rabbis; they have no official approval, no certificates, so to speak; so they're not allowed to handle the word of God in the Temple. But the authorities are also upset because of *what* they were teaching. The apostles are proclaiming in Jesus the resurrection of the dead. Not just Jesus' own resurrection, but in Jesus the general resurrection of the dead.

So they seize Peter and John and arrest them. Immediately Peter and John's lives are turned upside down. Peter was a fisherman; he spent three years with Jesus and the others. After the crucifixion he went back to fishing. He met with Jesus again and left fishing once more. He finds himself, filled with the Spirit, a healer and preacher in Jerusalem and now he's thrown into prison. If you want a quiet life, don't follow Jesus!

Imprisoned, they must wait until the next day for a hearing. It looks disastrous for them. But there's a vital lesson for anybody who ever experiences any form of persecution, however civil and polite it might be, because of proclaiming the gospel of God. Look at what has happened through the preaching. In a wonderful bit of storytelling, Luke gives us the picture of Peter and John being seized, hauled off, slammed in jail and thus silenced. But meanwhile the number of men who believe grows to about five thousand. They can arrest the preacher; but they cannot stop the word of life. As Luther put it in his hymn *A Safe Stronghold*.

Although they take our life,
Goods, honour, children, wife,
Yet is their profit small:
These things shall vanish all,
The city of God remaineth.

Morning brings the arrival of the heavyweights. 'The next day the rulers, elders and teachers of the law met in Jerusalem. Annas the high priest was there, and so were Caiaphas, John, Alexander and the other men of the high priest's family' (Acts 4:5,6).

Where have we come across them before in the story of God's mission to build his kingdom? They were the ones before whom Jesus had been illegally tried. The rulers were the priests on the Sanhedrin; the elders were lay-leaders, heads of the significant families, Israel's aristocracy; and the teachers of the law (or, as they are sometimes called, the scribes) were the legal experts in the Pharisees' party. These were the authorities that comprised the Sanhedrin. Notice that these are human agencies. But as rebel worldlings they are only providing a front for the one who is the source of the rebellion; the devil. They are a front for the one who failed with Jesus but who would try everything he can with his church. Satan's back was broken by the cross and the resurrection, yet he still vents his fury and malicious madness upon the people of God. It is the picture of Satan at work that we have in Revelation 12. Satan, enraged because he has not been able to devour the child that was born of God's people, pours out his madness upon the church and pursues her in an attempt to devour her instead.

We took note of the content of Peter and John's teaching: the resurrection. The Sadducees didn't believe in any kind of resurrection for anyone. The priests certainly didn't want to accept the resurrection of Jesus because they wanted Jesus to be history: he was gaining unwelcome popularity, and the resurrection accused them of being woefully wrong. Yet they also recognise the power of the teaching in the lives of those who are listening. The preaching of this unschooled fisherman has the power to change people. They would have known that many believed at Pentecost. About three thousand were added to their number on that day. More had believed each day since then (Acts 2:47). They would have heard that despite locking up the preacher, the number of men who believed had now grown to about five thousand; all because of what Peter had been preaching in their Temple precincts. They recognised the content and denied it; they recognised the power, but could not deny that. Both were a clear threat to them.

That's one of the reasons why Satan will oppose anything that proclaims Jesus Christ. It's not just that he hates the content; he also hates and opposes the power of God. We need to recognise this for the sake of our own lives as God's fellow builders. Satan opposes not just the truth, but the power of God. He will do anything either to twist the content, so that we don't preach the resurrection, or to rob us of our dependence on the power of God so that we become ineffective. Why it is that sometimes we just clam up and don't want to say anything? Our habitual response is to blame ourselves and say, 'I'm a useless witness.' But that's not always true – we're not always as bad as the accuser would like us to believe. Who knows the power of God in the declaration of the gospel and so doesn't want you to speak? In whose best interests is it that we remain silent? It's not in ours or God's; it's in the devil's own best interest. So when we perpetuate our silence by telling ourselves that we can witness simply by our lives and need never actually say anything at all about Christ, we need to recognise that the 'voice' in our ears is the devil trying to gag us. The gospel is the power of God for salvation. So if the devil can't twist the content, he will silence the messengers. As long as this true and powerful word does not break out among the sinners, he'll be happy.

Peter's Response

How will Peter react? What does he say to these Christ-haters in this key moment in his life?

Luke, who painted the darkest picture of Peter's denials and collapse, now gives us the brightness of Peter's transformed life, for Peter had been around these people before. On the fateful night of Jesus' trial by this same group, Peter was down in the courtyard of the high priest's house. From there he could see Jesus being harangued by them. We know that he could see Jesus because when the cock crowed, Jesus looked straight at Peter and Peter saw the look. Peter was terrified of these powerful and violent enemies of his Lord and his courage had failed him: he denied Christ rather than face them. Now he's in front of them again: the same power-brokers who had arrested and tried Jesus and who had fixed it for him to be crucified. Imagine what would be going through his mind.

How many of us work in this way: if we fail once in a situation, we're more likely to fail again? For many of us, the way in which we respond the first time we come up against a problem or a crisis forms a mould for how we respond the next time. If we respond well we tend to gain confidence and do well again. If we respond badly the first time, we will have a tendency to respond badly again. The first time Peter had been before these same people, he'd denied Christ and broken down. He had witnessed the consequences for Jesus of standing up to them with integrity and courage. He knows the power that they can wield. He knows what can happen when you don't back down. Now he's before them again. But now he has courage. We see a completely different Peter. Yes, he could still speak first and think later, blurting out words with more haste than care. But he's no longer the Peter who had once bottled out; now he is Peter with courage.

Where does his courage come from? Certainly being a witness of the resurrection helps: it gives conviction. Peter has already demonstrated an aptitude for preaching which might lend him a kind of confidence. But these things are not enough to account for the courage that he shows here. We cannot account for it without regard to what Luke writes in Acts 4:8: 'Then Peter, filled with the Holy Spirit, said to them . . .' Peter is filled with the Spirit right there and then for the moment that God has created.

It's a relief to us, but also a challenge. The relief is that we are not required to be filled with our own self-confidence in order to be effective fellow-builders with God. God builds. Jesus said, 'I will build my church' and as he sent the Spirit into the lives of the believers then, so he sends his Spirit to us now. The strength is going to come from him, which should take away some of the fear that the devil sows. It should take away some of that sense of self-condemnation and panic that we often feel when, as Peter was here, we are cornered by those opposed to the king. We don't have to summon up courage from within ourselves. We don't have to revert to some kind of carnal self-confidence, based on either past experience or on learned techniques. We cannot trust ourselves, even our God-given personality and character. That's not to say that God doesn't use who we are and what we've learned – after all, he's made us and schooled us precisely so that he might glorify himself through us. But we can fail; as Peter had failed. We trust *God*. We need his Spirit all the time and will be supplied with the Spirit over and over again. We don't need to worry in advance about those whom we face, because when we face them, God will give us the courage we need. He is to be trusted for that. He's not out to make an idiot of you. He is not the kind of Father who abandons his children when they need him

the most. Peter has courage because he is filled with the
Spirit; and the Spirit isn't scared of anyone.

What's Peter's answer to the charges? He preaches
Christ again, just exactly as he had done earlier. Notice
that he doesn't alter the message one bit. He is a witness:
the facts haven't changed, so neither does the message.
This is another thing that we need to have clear in our
minds about building the kingdom of God: all through
the book of Acts God uses fellow-builders who simply
witness to him. A witness does not have control of the
message. The witness says what they saw. The witness is
not there to make up a story that they think will produce
the right effect. A witness, by definition, just tells it like it
is. God uses us when we tell it like it is. We do it in
different ways and with different styles; different gifts
and aptitudes are deployed around different bits of the
building site. But no fellow-builder is called upon to
control the gospel and shape the building to suit their
own taste or their own ends.

As Peter answers, he repeats what he had said to the
crowd about how the man was healed. There he had said
that it was done in the power of Jesus Christ of Nazareth,
and here he says the same:

> 'Rulers and elders of the people! If we are being called to
> account today for an act of kindness shown to a cripple,
> and are asked how he was healed, then know this, you and
> all the people of Israel: It is by the name of Jesus Christ of
> Nazareth, whom you crucified but whom God raised from
> the dead, that this man stands before you healed' (4:8–10).

Amazing! Peter is speaking to the men who arranged
Jesus' crucifixion, and he echoes through the gathering
the terms of the charge that hung over Jesus' head when
he was on the cross: INRI – Jesus of Nazareth, king of the

Jews. If you wanted to call Jesus anything that would be absolutely guaranteed to get up the collective nose of the Sanhedrin, then you would call him Jesus, the anointed One (Christ), of Nazareth. It offended their theology, it threatened their power-play and it pierced their consciences. And just in case any of them had failed to recognise the allusion, Peter the Unsubtle (well, he did come from the geographical and cultural equivalent of Yorkshire!) presses the point home: 'By Jesus Christ of Nazareth, whom you crucified, but whom God raised from the dead, this man stands before you healed.'

He nails them. With hammer blows of truth he fastens their own guilt upon them. This true-hearted fellow-builder of God's kingdom talks to them about being builders. Irony of ironies, they thought they were building a kingdom for God. But what had happened? They had done precisely what God's fellow-builders must not do: they had taken control of the word of God. Instead of being witnesses to what God gave through Moses and the prophets, these people on the Sanhedrin had become the controllers. They had already shaped the message by adding 'the traditions of men', as Jesus had called them in Mark 7:8. Now they were editing out Jesus and the resurrection. And they tried to enforce their message with their power, with their authority, with their rules, even with their Temple police. There's nothing among the Sanhedrin about trusting in the power of God.

Peter uses the language of building with stinging irony. The authorities that he stands before are what builders should never be and they do the things that builders should never do. They can never be God's fellow-builders. On the contrary, 'The stone you builders rejected . . . has become the capstone' (verse 11). He really does let them have it with both barrels. Yet he never simply blasts them in a self-indulgent rant: he honours the name of Jesus Christ. 'Salvation is found in no-one else, for there is no other name under heaven given to men by which we must be saved' (verse 12). The authorities have names, of course. They appeal to 'Moses' and 'Abraham'. Thinking that they obey the law of Moses, and being able to trace their family trees back to Abraham, they think that they are saved. But 'No!' says Peter, 'Salvation is found in no-one else, for there is no other name under heaven given to men by which we must be saved.'

Peter's Impact

The courage of the apostles has enormous impact. So does the message itself. It dawns on some of the council members that having the courage to proclaim this message so boldly has to do with the fact that Peter and John have been with Jesus. The preaching is already beginning to have a deflating effect upon the Sanhedrin. They can't argue against Peter; they have to acknowledge the effect of Jesus and they can't deny the healing because the man is standing there. But they won't accept the consequences of any of it either.

There may well be people, to whom we bear clear and courageous witness, who will back down from their opposition to us and to what we are saying. They might find that they can no longer argue against us because they see a changed life. It might be ours, it might be somebody else's, but still they will not accept the consequences. You can go a long, long way down the religious line and never get to the station. It's not the fault of the fellow-builders – be encouraged! It's in the hardness of the heart of those who are receiving that witness.

Yet though the opposers cannot think of an answer, they still try to stop the proclamation of the message. Demonstrating a remarkable ability not to learn, and in a lame attempt to recover the situation, they say (verse 17) 'We must warn these men to speak no longer to anyone in this name.'

But these men neither fear you nor obey you! If they did, they wouldn't have been teaching in the Temple in the first place. If he feared and obeyed you, Peter wouldn't have stood up and said, 'You crucified him whom God raised from the dead. You are opposed to God. God is opposed to you.' As they shrink before the power of God, Peter fires off his disdainful retort: 'Judge for yourselves whether it is right in God's sight to obey you rather than God.'

Notice not only the content and the courage, but a great deal of cleverness. Peter is an unskilled fisherman. Where did he get the ability to reply like that? He is filled with the Spirit and the Spirit is much cleverer than the Sanhedrin. We sometimes wonder, 'What will I say when somebody asks me a question?' Because we are worried about not knowing the answers, we tend to fear and avoid situations in which people are likely to ask questions. Of course, there are things we can do to prepare and to know our stuff. And we can always say 'I don't know, but I'll find out.' But it is not beyond the power of the Spirit to give you an answer that you couldn't have thought of yourself in a month of Sundays, the appropriateness and effectiveness of which you could never have worked out. The Spirit is with you, in you. God equips his fellow-builders, not just with the raw materials – the gospel that is to be proclaimed; nor just with courage and power: he also gives savvy. Back to the building site: he can give you the instinct to know where to put such and such a stone and which bits to chisel off this bit to make it fit with that one. God gives the savvy to build well and wisely.

The Sanhedrin has no answer. How can they come up with a reply to that? They are caught, just as Jesus so brilliantly caught the scribes time after time. They can't even decide how to punish Peter and John. They make a few threats to save face; what else can they do? All the people are there and are praising God; these priests and religious people are supposed to encourage people to praise God, so they're well and truly stuck. What can they do but let them go?

God 1, Sanhedrin 0.

The Emerging Pattern

Religious resistance

Before we move on, we need to note another element of the emerging pattern. We've already seen that we, worked within, work the works of God. We've also seen that Peter seizes the moments that God creates, and so must we. But we also notice this: religious resistance, by which I mean resistance from those who have concocted their own way of being right with God. It's not the resistance of those who do not believe in God. It is the resistance of those who say to themselves, 'I'm all right, Jack. I can do this salvation thing for myself.' It comes out in a multitude of ways: 'I can make it all right with the man upstairs. It'll all come out in the wash. I've been good most of my life and the good things will outweigh the bad things. I've always tried to do my best and I've never hurt anyone. I've been to church, and given to charity. I've been a good husband and I've tried to be a good father.' Such are the gospels that people write for themselves. That's what I mean by religious resistance. It is the hardest resistance that we will encounter, whether

it comes from people who think they are Christians or
from people who have another religion or from those
who simply think they are decent citizens. It is the
hardest resistance that we will encounter because there is
no room in it for a sense of guilt before God, nor for
remorse or repentance. There is no room in it for a sense
of needing a Saviour. There is no room in it to respond to
the unconditional love of God. That religious resistance
brings its costs for us when the true gospel confronts it.
There is a price that we have to pay. May the Lord
encourage and help us in this. We are called to proclaim
the gospel with courage, by the power of God and as we
are constantly filled with his Spirit to cope with the
situations he places us in. It will have impact; part of that
impact might be to raise opposition and to deepen the
resistance of those who are proud before God.

But we take this to heart: did opposition daunt Peter
and John? Did it dissuade them from being fellow-
builders? Not for a moment! They couldn't help it. 'We
cannot help speaking about what we have seen and
heard' (verse 20). They take the knocks yet they cannot
but stand up again and carry on. God's fellow-builders
are persistent. They have a stick-ability that does not
come from themselves; it comes from God. In our
witness, as in our conduct generally, we resist the enemy
who would silence us. Our calling, in Paul's words in 1
Corinthians 15:58, is to stand firm, letting nothing move
us, always giving ourselves fully to the work of the Lord,
because we know that our labour in the Lord is not in
vain.

To ponder

● Cost-free Christianity? What has yours cost you
  recently? Do you regret it or, as you look back, does

your loss seem like gain? If you can't think of it costing you anything, what does that say?

- Do you tend to relate to God as if he is mostly the Great Provider or mostly the Great Demander? Do you resent him for anything? Can you tell him this?
- How does people's opposition to the king show itself in those spheres of your life that you thought of at the end of the last chapter? How about the decent, friendly, happy non-Christians that you know: how does their opposition show?
- What can you do or say to show merely religious friends that religion is no substitute for a relationship with God?

Chapter 3

Peter, Cornelius and God's Big Issue

We're sticking with Peter, so we've jumped to Acts chapter 10 and particularly verses 9 to 48. We'll back-track later and look at Stephen. We will also look at Philip, whose encounter with the Ethiopian eunuch is crucial in the overall plot of the book of Acts; the plot being the spread of the gospel's living flame from Jerusalem out to the world.

The missing episodes include martyrdom, persecution and the scattering of the church. By these traumatic events, the church grew. Quite the opposite of what we would think. We would think the church would grow more where it's successful and safe. But God did it differently: the church grew when it was, from a human perspective, extremely unsafe. A message on the back of an Operation Mobilisation worker's T-shirt read, 'A ship is safe and comfortable in the harbour. But that's not what ships are for.' The harbour – Jerusalem – ceased to be safe anyway; but the church was never meant to stay in Jerusalem. The plan was to go to the ends of the earth.

We have also missed out God's big shocker. It really was, in terms of personnel, the biggest surprise imaginable. Nobody could have anticipated that the headlines in the *Jerusalem Christian Times* would read 'Saul of Tarsus Saved'.

For now, though, we follow the work of God in the former fisherman, whose lessons in a different kind of fishing are far from over. Like Philip's witness to the Ethiopian, the meeting of Jewish Peter and Gentile Cornelius also has a strategic significance in the story of the building of God's kingdom. Precisely because of this, the question of what God had to do in Peter's life to work with him is vital. As we'll see, when God could have used an angel, he used Peter instead and in order to do so, did profound work in Peter's life. Again!

Cornelius and Peter

The story takes us to the bustling, prosperous sea-port of Caesarea. A Roman garrison, Caesarea was a safe and secure administrative base and was a key centre from which to proclaim the gospel. But there is more to Acts 10 than the arrival of the gospel in a geographically strategic location.

Cornelius, a centurion in the Italian Regiment, has turned away from the pagan religions of Rome, especially those of the soldiers. This Gentile has loosely connected himself with aspects of Jewish religion that we came across earlier: praying regularly and giving generously to those in need. He is devout, he lives an upright life and he is known for it. He has selected like-minded soldiers to work with him closely in his household.

But Cornelius and his household have not yet heard the gospel. Cue Peter. As Cornelius is praying, an angel appears to Cornelius and tells him to send men to Joppa, for along the coast is a man named Simon who is called Peter, who is staying with another Simon, the tanner, whose house is by the sea.

It's relevant to the main thread running through this book that Cornelius had to send for Peter. Think of it – the angel could have told Cornelius the gospel right there and then. The angel would have done it perfectly: the right words in the right order, spoken with glory, with angelic authority and power. But evidently, the simple communication of the message was not the only item on God's agenda. God is not simply spreading a message; he is – throughout all his kingdom-building – shaping his fellow-builders. God wanted to use Peter, not because Peter could utter an evangelistic message more brilliantly than an angel, but because Peter had to change. For him to develop as a fellow-builder with God, Peter's horizons had to enlarge to reach the vast extent of God's mission. The immediate work with Cornelius required it, but the further development of the church was soon – by the time we reach Acts 15 – to depend on Peter's first-hand experience of the fact that God's grace is global.

God's Big Issue

This incident is crucial in the progress of God's great plan to redeem a people to himself from all nations. Saul's conversion and commission to be the apostle to the Gentiles and Peter's involvement with Cornelius are critical processes in the gospel going out to all nations. For Peter and others in the church in Jerusalem, God's plan was going to require a change in their doctrine away from a view of Christianity that was still heavily encrusted with Judaism. It was also going to require a change in their practice. God was going to mix them with people that up until now they had religiously avoided. These changes would demand a reassessment of the party lines in the early church. The church has always had its groupings and affiliations. But the gospel was for all nations because nothing less than that would glorify God: he had made the world.

As we took note of earlier, that phrase 'all nations' runs right through the Old Testament, starting with God's call to Abraham, 'Through your seed all nations will be blessed.' Like a stream, the human line that will lead to the 'seed' flows down from Abraham to Isaac to Jacob; it narrows from a nation to one tribe: Judah. It follows through to one little clan in a triflingly small town, Bethlehem, and winds its almost disappearing way down the years until it trickles into the birth of just one person, Jesus Christ. While the line of Abraham's 'seed' narrows down, the scope of God's gospel has always been a mile wide. We see its breadth in the covenant promise to Abraham, but also in later passages such as Isaiah chapter 2, and in his amazing closing prophecies, particularly chapters 65 and 66.

Small wonder, then, that Jesus expressed the global scope of God's saving plan in the commissions that he gave to the disciples in Matthew 28 and Luke 24. The gospel is to be taken from that one man who is God, to all nations. It was also part of the commission that came in Acts chapter 1:8 'you will receive power when the Holy Spirit comes upon you, and you will be my witnesses in Jerusalem, and in all Judea and Samaria, and to the ends of the earth'.

It is in this vast building work that you and I are made participants by grace. It will reach its completion, for in the book of Revelation we are given the sight of heaven, where there will be a multitude of redeemed men and women that no-one can count, from every tribe, language, people and nation (Rev. 5:9, 7:9).

Up until his encounter with God and Cornelius, Peter had never understood how big God's house was intended to be. So in Acts 10 God confronts this converted Jew with the big issue: the gospel is for the Gentiles too.

Peter Needs a Lesson

You cannot be serious!

Before Peter is going to be effective, he needs to learn. In some respects, that's one of the main things we need to take in from this episode in his life. A huge hole is about to open up in his understanding of the mission of God and thereby his own mission. Into that void God will pour his truth, not (interestingly, for those of us with a 'teaching ministry') by sitting Peter down with the relevant texts, but by confronting him with the experience of the truth. Peter learns his lesson and he learns it well; and we see more of the emerging pattern of how God uses his fellow-builders.

In fact, Peter needs not one but three lessons. He needs a lesson in doctrine, but he also needs an inward lesson: an attitude lesson. God will always teach us these two, because his word is never personally or pastorally neutral. He never expects to be listened to disinterestedly, as if he is just one voice in an after-dinner conversation at the theology club. Not just what we think, but *how* we think – our logic, our frame of mind, our fears and hopes, hates and loves – these are all to be transformed by God. Listen to a Bible-teaching ministry or open the pages of the Bible yourself and expect not just to be given new information, but to be taught the attitude lessons. And just as God's word is not neutral as far as our attitudes are concerned, so it is not neutral with respect to our behaviour. So we should expect (and positively look for) a third kind of lesson: the 'action' lesson. We ask, 'What do I need to *do* about this, Lord?'

The three kinds of lesson might not come in that order, clearly they didn't for Peter here – he had to do something in response to a command that didn't make sense; and then he had to think about it, so that his understanding and attitude changed; then he could do the new obedience. But whatever the order, thought, attitude, and action must all yield to the Lordship of Christ and so glorify him who constantly addresses us.

Peter's attitude problem runs deep. It's one that we can identify with and it can have profound repercussions for our participation in God's mission. Put simply, Peter thinks he knows better than God. In fact, we might say that Peter *still* thinks he knows better than God, despite his earlier experience in the other Caesarea, during his time with Jesus. Jesus gave Peter a painfully sharp rebuke, after Peter had said 'You are the Christ, the Son of the living God' – the staggering and God-given acknowledgement of the supremacy of Christ. His next contribution, made with reference to the cross, is 'No, Lord, never' – for which read, 'I know better than you.' Jesus had fired back the rebuke: 'Get behind me, Satan.' It wasn't that Jesus thought that Peter was actually Satan, but Jesus saw that Satan was manipulating Peter into being against the cross, the cross which was Jesus' purpose and his glory.

The same basic issue surfaces now in Joppa, though this time it looks as though it has to do with what the righteous may or may not eat. When it comes to the finer points of religion, Peter knows better than God!

Peter is on the roof, cooled by the sea breeze, praying. He might not be perfect, but in his life the prayerful devotion of the Son is being repeated. He has a vision of a sheet being lowered and on it is food. It's not ready to be eaten yet: it's a little too mobile for most palates! There's the small matter of selecting and killing it. Before Peter can choose what to eat, God gives a command – not a 'serving suggestion' but a straight command.

As far as Peter is concerned, it really is a repulsive command that God gives. It might not seem so to our Gentile minds, but for Peter, at this stage in his life, it is a vile and shocking thing that God tells him to do. It's understandable that Peter reacts as he does. When God told Peter to 'Get up, kill and eat', it went against everything that he had ever been taught from God's own law. As Peter had grown up, trying to be a good Jew, performing all the Jewish religious observances and trying to keep himself ceremonially clean, he would have learned, and had it repeatedly reinforced, that certain animals were forbidden. They were forbidden by the very One who now tells him to eat them. There is no differentiation in God's command to him on the roof-top between those 'clean' animals that are okay to eat, the ones that chew the cud, and the 'unclean' ones that Jews were not supposed to eat.

This is a huge shift to ask of Peter. In terms of his religion, culture and personal practice, it is a complete reversal of everything he'd heard from those scrolls of the law that had been opened up and read in the synagogue. He instinctively stuck to the natural, literal and accepted reading of the Scriptures. If he'd had the right scroll with him on the roof top, he'd have been able to point out to God exactly where God himself had said *not* to eat these things.

So Peter comes out with the self-contradicting attitude that he'd shown once before; 'No way, Lord!' How can you say 'No way' and 'Lord' in the same sentence? One of the terms has to give way to the other: you can't have both. Peter had forgotten the rebuke that he had received when he had tried to put God right the first time. His reply pre-echoes the most memorable phrase that the hallowed courts of Wimbledon have ever heard from a tennis player: 'You cannot be serious!'

Never one to do things by halves, Peter compounds his trouble by declaring his righteousness to God. Effectively, Peter says, 'And by the way, Lord, don't you know how righteous I am? You're not asking some sort of compromised backslider who'll eat anything he finds in the street. I have *never* ever eaten *anything* impure or unclean. I'm a righteous man. Your command's a big enough hurdle for anybody, but for someone as righteous as me it really is too much' (pause while he recovers his equilibrium, then with renewed reverence) 'Lord.'

But whatever happened to a righteousness that comes by faith? Peter, do you think that you *ever* made yourself clean or right with God by eating or not eating certain foods? What happened, Peter, to justification by faith?

Of course, Peter hadn't read all of Paul's epistles. (I'm being ironic here – Paul hadn't written any of them yet!) He didn't have the kind of full-blown doctrine of justification by faith that we can learn. But he knew that you live by faith in Jesus Christ: he had preached it. Now, when he is being not only religiously but culturally challenged, he reverts to religious and cultural type and he pleads righteousness by works.

But it gets worse. Not only has he flipped back into a cultural mode, but he has forgotten something else that happened with him and Jesus and the others. We recall Mark 7:14,15. The Pharisees have raised precisely this issue of 'clean' and 'unclean' foods. They have been grilling Jesus over his disciples, and Jesus has rebuked them in Mark 7:6,8, 'You hypocrites . . . you have let go of the commands of God and are holding on to the traditions of men' – an absolutely pivotal phrase in the gospels. (Later the principle would be equally pivotal in Paul's encounter with Judaisers and legalists. It still echoes as a word of rebuke to many of us in the church.) Jesus has gone on to speak to them and then to the crowd who are listening, and, of course, to the disciples. We know that they are listening, because they ask him about it. Then we read from verse 14; 'Jesus called the crowd to him and said, "Listen to me, everyone, and understand this. Nothing outside a man can make him 'unclean' by going into him. Rather, it is what comes out of a man that makes him 'unclean'."'

It's not what you take in, since that goes into your stomach and then through you; it's what comes out from your heart. It's your heart, it's your will, it's your disposition to do this and not that – it's your heart and what comes out of it that renders you clean or unclean before God. Of course for clean and unclean we read 'acceptable' or 'unacceptable' to God. It's not something you take in, it's something in you. As the saying goes, we are not sinners because we sin; we sin because we are sinners. The problem of uncleanness lies in the heart, not on the plate.

> After had left the crowd and entered the house, his disciples asked him about this parable. 'Are you so dull?' he asked. 'Don't you see that nothing that enters a man from the outside can make him "unclean"? For it doesn't go into his heart but into his stomach, and then out of his body.' (In saying this, Jesus declared all food clean.) He went on: 'What comes out of a man is what makes him "unclean". For from within, out of men's hearts, come evil thoughts, sexual immorality, theft, murder, adultery, greed, malice, deceit, lewdness, envy, slander, arrogance and folly' (Mk. 7:17–22).

It's a disorder common to the religiously minded to worry about small details of conduct. We'll hone our scruples about superficialities but barely notice or address the vileness that can come from the depths of our hearts. We can become self-righteously pernickety over meetings, wearing the approved kinds of clothes, using the right phrases, or never letting a naughty word slip out. But we fail to make any fuss over greed, envy, bitterness or grudge-bearing. The most fastidious can be the least gracious. We can be perfectionists when it comes to the codes of conduct in our groups, but our self-centredness means that we'll hardly bat an eyelid at the plight of the homeless in our inner cities or the starving in famine-stricken countries overseas. We'll reduce our relationship with God to manageable externals so that we needn't feel bad about the inner evil that infests our whole beings, so that we needn't face the utter bankruptcy of our souls. We tinker religiously with the details of our visible conduct so that we needn't bow down and plead for mercy – mercy which God is immeasurably willing to show us. 'All these evils come from inside and make a man "unclean"' (Mk. 7:23).

God Teaches Patiently

Not once, not twice, but ...

Peter had a vital lesson to learn if he was going to be the fellow-builder that God had called him to be. So God teaches patiently. After Peter's first reply, 'The voice spoke to him a second time, "Do not call anything impure that God has made clean." This happened three times' (Acts 10:15,16).

Not once, not twice, but three times. God's fellow-builders need lessons to be taught, retaught, and retaught again. For many of us even three times isn't enough. Like the disciples, we can be so dull; and even when we have been taught again and again we can forget as Peter had forgotten. We don't catch it. The lessons go in one ear, hover around long enough to leave a vague trace upon our memories, and then fly out of the other ear. We should be patient with one another. God is a patient teacher.

At least Peter is thinking about the meaning of the vision. His brain has at least engaged first gear. He ponders the vision. In fact, he mulls it over so much and is so absorbed by what this vision means that he doesn't notice three men outside on the street, one of whom is a Roman soldier, yelling out so that everyone could hear, asking if Simon, known as Peter, was staying there.

He's so like us: a marvellous mixture. God uses some of the most complicated fellow-builders imaginable: eager, faithful, capable of massive failures, slow to learn, quick to forget, receptive of that power of the Spirit to enable him to preach, resistant to the truth; bold and timid. What a complex knot of traits, yet not a problem for God at all. As the children's song put it, 'Our God is a great big God'. He is a wonderful God, who, in his bigness, effortlessly takes our complexities and inconsistencies in his stride.

To his great credit, Peter will do what the Spirit says even though it is something simple. It is the next simple step that's going to have such profound consequences for Peter and the building of the kingdom. We sometimes wish that the Spirit would give us something spectacular to do. Mundane obedience seems pedestrian and unspiritual. But the Spirit simply says to Peter, 'Simon, three men are looking for you, so get up and go downstairs.' Remember how, when Naaman was told to go and dip in the Jordan, he protested that this was too simple, and besides, the Jordan was a filthy river? If he'd been given some spectacular and heroic challenge, he would have risen to it. It would have appealed to the flesh; he could have congratulated himself; he could have maintained his carnal dignity. How much more difficult it is to obey the prompting and nudging of the Spirit when it's something really simple like putting your head round the door at work and saying 'Hello' to somebody, or going across the floor of the church and speaking to somebody who is on their own. ('Quick, do it before they leave!') How difficult for us when the Spirit asks for something as simple as a smile.

In all this teaching and prompting, there is a point for some of us to take to heart: it's okay not to know everything. I don't mean that ignorance is virtuous, in a cutsey kind of way. What I mean is that it's not a problem to God that we, who are his fellow-builders, do not know everything. In fact, it's positively advantageous that we neither pretend that we know more than we do, nor bring to him our carnal expertise as if we were doing the One who knows the end from the beginning a favour. In fact, we can go as far as to say that it is a pre-requisite of being a fellow builder with God that we *know* that we don't know everything. It is vital that we *know* that we can be thick and forgetful and that we *know* that we need to learn; it's essential that we do *not* secretly harbour the notion that, actually, we are a bit of a dab hand at building and that we do *not* modestly pride ourselves on having mastered everything that can be done with granite and concrete and a chisel, thank you very much. Knowing that we don't know it all is a pre-requisite for the walk of faith.

As I've hinted, God required of Peter a complete turn around. God was about to engage Peter in the ministry to Cornelius and his family and household. Before long,

God would need him to engage with the apostles and brothers who were based back in Jerusalem, in conversations fraught with opportunity for disaster, but which would successfully pave the way for the work among the Gentiles through Paul. For these building tasks, God was going to require that Peter unlearn vast tracts of what he had been taught. And it wasn't just about food, which of course was simply the visual aid.

Peter had been brought up to think that not just certain edible animals but that also certain *people* were either clean and unclean; and that you should have absolutely nothing to do with unclean people or you too would become unclean. So, as plain as plain could be, the Spirit who was promised by Jesus and who had been poured out in the latter days that Joel had prophesied about and that Pentecost had ushered in, *this* Spirit couldn't have *anything* to do with those who were unclean. So if you were going to be a means of God's grace and forgiveness being poured out upon the unclean, it was for the unclean to make themselves clean before they could come within reach of your righteousness. In fact, you had to become part of the community of Israel in order to come into the sphere of justification. Only in the sphere of God's people, the Jews, could you receive justification. Outside that community you couldn't receive the Spirit, you couldn't receive justification or forgiveness. With that kind of mind-set, Peter the Christian not only wouldn't, he *couldn't* have anything to do with unclean Cornelius.

So everything had to change.

Some of us, if we are actually going to be God's fellow-builders, might need a similarly massive revolution in our thinking. Maybe we have precisely this turn-around to make, or at least a parallel one. Do we not wait for unclean non-Christians to clean up their acts sufficiently to come into a church? (Ugh! She *smokes*!) They need to become like us (quit smoking, and swearing as well for that matter, and while you're at it, God'll be much more interested in you if you drank less of an evening). They need to sit still, without questioning, 'under' sound preaching in a church, because here in church is where the Spirit is working, here in our church is where the preaching is done. They've got to clean up, come in and become like us in order to become one of us in our cosy relationship with our God. Of course the preaching is needed – this is Acts that we're looking at. The problem is in our attitude to the 'unclean': virtuously disgusted, vastly distanced.

Peter had to be turned inside out. He had to understand, and act upon the understanding, that God had a much, much bigger vision and that God could go and prepare people for the gospel without them first becoming 'clean'. In Peter's own hearing, Jesus had called all foods clean. God had to remind Peter that the question of acceptability lies with God and not with Peter. Peter had to learn that God could do all the preparatory work 'out there' among the Gentiles, as he had already been doing in Cornelius' life.

Even builders need to learn new things, and need to learn them from the Master Builder. To be good fellow-builders we must be teachable at precisely this point of reaching 'unclean' people with the gospel. It is our calling to 'hold out the word of life' as Paul put it to the Philippians (who were getting it right!) rather than to sit back and say, 'You come to us, and if you don't, you just prove more of your uncleanness, and we're absolutely justified in not having anything to do with you.' Recall the principle that Paul had worked with: 'I have become all things to all men so that by all possible means I might save some' (1 Cor. 9:22). Peter had been terminally unclean but his religious background hadn't taught him to see that. His baggage still made it difficult for him to register it deeply concerning himself. Yet grace is grace. If God could save Peter by grace, he could save anyone. If God's grace can reach and rescue me, God can save anyone.

Peter Learns the Lesson Well

At some point the penny drops and Peter realises that God isn't actually going on about what to eat when he is hungry; all that business about food is true but not the main point. The meaning of the vision comes to him; he grasps the truth and now he's going to run with it. He readily goes along with the messengers and the following day arrives in Caesarea. Cornelius is expecting him, has called together his relatives and close friends and ... don't blink or you'll miss this one ... Peter enters his house. It seems a small matter to us, almost a bit of story-telling that merely paints a picture of the scene: 'as Peter entered the house'. But crossing that threshold was enormously significant.

Peter goes into the house of a Gentile 'dog'. The teaching from the rabbis, which Peter would have grown up with, was that the Gentiles had been made to fuel the fires of hell. That's the only reason why God had made Gentiles. They were inherently unclean, like dogs. You wouldn't touch a dog, and you wouldn't go into the house of a Gentile. Even less so if he is also a Roman soldier, part of the occupying force. That Peter went in demonstrates how quickly he had learned the lesson: by doing this, as he makes clear in verses 28 and 29, he was making himself unclean. Now he was putting himself into what, on just the previous day, he would have abhorred as the unclean camp.

We have already seen how Peter had confronted religious resistance to the gospel. But in this incident, Peter has to confront it not in those who are aggressively against him, but in a much more difficult place. This time it does not come from the Sanhedrin, it comes from his own heart and mind. For some of us in the church, this is immensely challenging. We become so judgemental toward non-Christians. We develop a supposedly righteous dislike of sinners. Have we forgotten that we are still sinners, saved by grace alone? Do we stand in judgement on sinners, we who are sinners also and yet who have been regarded with such grace by the Holy One? It's so easy to turn into a spiritual snob. But how then can we dare to call Jesus, who left the brilliant holiness of heaven to die on an accursed cross for spiritual wretches like us, our *Lord*? What's our behaviour like towards those that we find disgustingly unrighteous? We tend to bristle a bit. Disapproval seeps from our faces. The body language gives us away. They're not good enough to be in our company. Not our sort. What a mercy for us that God doesn't think like that.

What sea-change needs to happen in the oceans of your heart? The change begins, I think, with a sense of our sin and with a corresponding gratitude that we are forgiven. If we don't think we're all that bad, we won't feel all that thankful that we've been forgiven. Neither will we love God that much for what he's done. Disbelief concerning our own wickedness, secretly harbouring the thought that we ought to have been forgiven, ingratitude, lovelessness – these currents of the soul carry us away from genuine closeness to other sinners.

As Jesus had obeyed the Father, so now Peter obeys God rather than men, which was the riposte he had given to the Sanhedrin earlier when he was hauled before them after the healing of the man at the Gate Beautiful. Now he obeys the living word of God rather than the dead traditions of men. Another piece of the work of Christ is being refashioned in Peter. He is prepared to cut against the grain of many in the rest of the church. It's not because he is a maverick with a predisposition to make trouble. He's not that kind of man. Neither is he disobeying the traditions of men because he's arrogant. He is not an arrogant man. It's because the truth, which has been taught to him by the One who not only has truth to teach but who also, by his Spirit, makes us teachable, is more compelling than the traditions. The truth is more active and more authoritative. And this causes him to follow God even if it means pushing back the boundaries that enclose his brothers and sisters in Christ who are back in Jerusalem. He has gone against the cultural norm that prevailed even among his own brothers and sisters in Christ.

That's a risky thing for us to do. We risk losing friends by inviting their scorn. We risk being pulled by the world into its shape, conforming to its patterns, albeit in order to gain a hearing, and thereby losing the distinctiveness of our Christian identity. We entertain a suspicion that the 'all things to all men' principle is actually a bad thing, the description of a compromised believer. ('Didn't he stand up for *anything*?') We also risk losing the plot ourselves: there's something that appeals to some of us about being not simply different from other Christians, but actually better. We shift our focus from testifying to Christ to belittling fellow-Christians, behaving as if the main point of our lives were to protest at our churches. While breaking out of the boundaries can be a matter of humble obedience to Christ, it can also be a matter of pride: we're better than the poor unenlightened souls who still go to church. Risk induces fear. These fears – of losing friends or of compromising our integrity or of acting out of vain conceit – cripple us when it comes to carrying the gospel over the thresholds of our religious comfort zones and into the world.

Peter didn't just cross the threshold into Cornelius's house; he crossed the evangelistic Rubicon that day. There would be no going back. He took the gospel to a place that was, in cultural and religious terms, as barren and remote as the moon. (You can see this next line coming, can't you? 'That was one small step for a man, one giant leap for the gospel'!)

And yet, Peter has retained his humility. 'As Peter entered his house, Cornelius met him and fell at his feet in reverence. But Peter made him get up. "Stand up," he said, "I am only a man myself" ' (verses 25,26). There's no vanity in the man at all. He doesn't hesitate over this; he doesn't bask in the adulation even for a split second. He has humility, simplicity and sense. 'I'm only a man myself.'

Cornelius tells him what has happened and clearly the Lord has been preparing the ground wonderfully. God had let himself into Cornelius's home before the angel came knocking or before Cornelius opened the door to Peter. God's fellow-builders never start from scratch and then bring him in to what he is doing. It is always a matter of God calling us in on his work. He is always the pioneer missionary. He is always the church planter. He is always the evangelist, who gets there before we ever do. So many of our struggles in the church have to do with us not catching up with God, with us not discerning and following God's work but having many jobs of our own which we then ask God to bless. We get the whole thing on its head. We even talk in prayer meetings about bringing the Lord in on a situation. Whose universe is this? When do we ever have to bring God in on a situation? God constantly has to bring us in on his work.

Think of it in terms of the workplace. Do you have to bring God in on the people at work, as if he's locked out of the office, the staffroom or the ward? Does he sit in heaven, inactively but patiently waiting for Carol and Dave, who are the only two Christians in the place, to get the witnessing going to such a point that they'll need him? The 'good conversations' with Frank from Accounts have reached a level where God's going to have to do something; so Carol gets her church prayer meeting, and Dave his cell-group, to pray that God will come in and 'do it' for Frank. But God has been working away in Frank's life for years! Frank's Gran was praying for him even before Carol was born. Three years before Dave became a Christian, Frank was given a New Testament at school and read bits of it that, curiously, have never gone away. And when Frank wakes in the middle of the night wondering if there's more to life than 'this', it's God who's whispering 'Yes.'

Peter does what he's done before. He seizes the moment. He doesn't talk about himself. He doesn't talk about how great it is to be an apostle. He doesn't play to the gallery. He preaches Christ. Yet although he preaches the same gospel, he preaches it in a different way. Before, when he spoke to the Sanhedrin, he was confrontational. But here is a completely different situation. These people don't need nailing. Neither did they know about Jesus and the things he did. So Peter isn't confrontational: he explains carefully who Jesus is.

You know what has happened throughout Judea, beginning in Galilee after the baptism that John preached – how God anointed Jesus of Nazareth with the Holy Spirit and power, and how he went around doing good and healing all who were under the power of the devil, because God was with him (Acts 10:37,38).

He's doing more than just passing on information; he's hooking right into where Cornelius is. Cornelius does good deeds: Jesus went about doing good. Cornelius knows that God is with him. So Peter, with skilful wisdom, talks to Cornelius about Jesus. God was with Jesus too. He tells Cornelius that God shows no favouritism but accepts men from every nation who fear him and do what is right – another hook into Cornelius's life. Peter opens Cornelius's heart to Christ and then lays at his feet God's good news and God's claim upon Cornelius's life: 'You know the message God sent to the people of Israel telling the good news of peace through Jesus Christ, who is Lord of all.' This message has come from God, Peter infers, it is not made up by us. This is what God wants us to know: the way to have peace with God and peace in your heart is through Jesus. This Jesus has a claim upon your life, because he isn't simply Lord of a few, he is Lord of all – all things, all places and all people. He is Lord over death, for he rose from the grave. And one day we will all have to answer to him.

Then what happens?

> While Peter was still speaking these words, the Holy Spirit came on all who heard the message. The circumcised believers who had come with Peter were astonished that the gift of the Holy Spirit had been poured out even on the Gentiles. For they heard them speaking in tongues and praising God (verses 44–46).

Notice what's said about the giving of the Spirit: the first thing that Luke records is that the gift is the Holy Spirit: not the gifts of the Spirit, but the Holy Spirit himself. The Spirit himself comes in life-imparting power. Up until now, Cornelius has had a measure of understanding but there has been no new life. So the Spirit is given to bring

Cornelius from his death in transgressions and sins to new life in Christ. Then the Spirit's presence is shown in the same way here as had been the case in Jerusalem. A kind of Gentile Pentecost happens.

This will have enormous significance for the building of the kingdom. When Peter and the others go back to Jerusalem to report on events in Caesarea, the fact that the same Spirit had done the same things in both places convinces the people back in Jerusalem that God has been at work among the Gentiles. But there's even more than a strategic advantage: something about the mission of God is being demonstrated in this Gentile Pentecost. The pouring out of the Spirit in Jerusalem had been a sign of the fulfilment of God's covenant in Christ. By pouring out the Holy Spirit on Gentiles, God is demonstrating that yes, the covenant is fulfilled for the Gentiles as well as for those who had previously thought themselves to be the only covenant people, the Jews.

It is pivotal work that God does *through* Peter in Caesarea. He did it because of the work that he had first done *in* Peter.

There's one more aspect of God's work in the fellow-builders here that is demonstrated with startling clarity. God requires his fellow-builders to catch up with him and his work, even when God's work is messy.

When Peter crosses the threshold of Cornelius's house and speaks about the forgiveness of sins through the name of Jesus Christ and when the Holy Spirit comes upon all who are gathered, God makes an untidy mess of what people had made neat. God creates more questions than answers; he disorders the customs, presuppositions and expectations of all who are there. How are these Gentiles, on whom the Holy Spirit is poured, going to worship? Are they going to worship like Jews? Are they going to worship like Jews who have become Christians? How are Jewish believers going to relate to them? How are these people, whom God is bringing into his new order, going to relate to their fellow-Romans? What will the implications be for Cornelius and his job? God creates so many questions. He disrupts so much that the early Christians had assumed. He throws away their cultural and theological control panels. He wrests power out of their hands and fills life with new uncertainties.

Why does God do this to us? Because we're on a building site and building sites are untidy and full of uncertainty. You don't get all the questions about the building answered until the work is finished. You have to wait and see. If you want something neat and tidy, wander round the show house, don't work on the building site. But of course, the show house isn't a real home. To discern the work and the will of God requires that we relinquish the comfort of being 'sorted', of being experts in the church. It requires us to rediscover the attitudes, the prayers, the Scriptures that belong to the world of disciples, rather than the world of experts. We are all on a journey; none of us has arrived yet, so we are listeners and learners. God is Lord, we are not. Thankfully.

To ponder

- Who are the most repulsive people that you can think of? (It might be an individual, rather than a group of people.) Do you really believe that God loves them as much as he loves you? How can you communicate the gospel to them?
- What is good about the people that you named in the set of questions at the end of chapter 1? How can their good qualities become a bridge to connect them with the truth about Christ?

- In what areas of your life have you experienced God helping you to catch up with what he's already been doing?
- Do you have a set of criteria that people have to meet before you will become interested in sharing the gospel with them? Perhaps they have to use some of our Christian jargon, or show some interest in coming to church, or stop swearing so much.
- Who are the people in your church whose opinions of you matter the most? Why do their opinions matter so much, and how much does that affect what you'll do with your time, or the level of your involvement in the lives of non-Christians?

Chapter 4

When Faithfulness Costs Your Life

The Life and Death of Stephen

In those days when the number of disciples was increasing, the Grecian Jews among them complained against the Hebraic Jews because their widows were being overlooked in the daily distribution of food. So the Twelve gathered all the disciples together and said, 'It would not be right for us to neglect the ministry of the word of God in order to wait on tables. Brothers, choose seven men from among you who are known to be full of the Spirit and wisdom. We will turn this responsibility over to them and will give our attention to prayer and the ministry of the word.' This proposal pleased the whole group. They chose Stephen, a man full of faith and of the Holy Spirit; also Philip, Procorus, Nicanor, Timon, Parmenas, and Nicolas from Antioch, a convert to Judaism. They presented these men to the apostles, who prayed and laid their hands on them. So the word of God spread. The number of disciples in Jerusalem increased rapidly, and a large number of priests became obedient to the faith. Now Stephen, a man full of God's grace and power, did great wonders and miraculous signs among the people. Opposition arose, however, from members of the Synagogue of the Freedmen (as it was called) – Jews of Cyrene and Alexandria as well as the provinces of Cilicia and Asia. These men began to argue with Stephen, but they could not stand up against his wisdom or the Spirit by whom he spoke. Then they secretly persuaded some men to say, 'We have heard Stephen speak words of blasphemy against Moses and against God.' So they stirred up the people and the elders and the teachers of the law. They seized Stephen and brought him before the Sanhedrin. They produced false witnesses, who testified, 'This fellow never stops speaking against this holy place and against the law. For we have heard him say that this Jesus of Nazareth will destroy this place and change the customs Moses handed down to us.' All who were sitting in the Sanhedrin looked intently at Stephen, and they saw that his face was like the face of an angel (Acts 6:1–15).

Being a Fellow-Builder is no Game

The flow of Acts slows around Stephen. By reducing the pace of the narrative, Luke invites us to pause and reflect on the man and on his witness. Stephen's story marks a qualitative shift in the church's understanding of life with Christ: it is the shift to death with Christ. These events turn God's fellow-builders' perception of their mission in an even more Christ-like direction. It will be costly to be a disciple in a way that it hasn't been yet. We have had arrests before but we have not had a death. No-one has had to give their life for the gospel. A marker is laid down here that the gospel and the growth of God's kingdom will cost not only the discomfort that goes along with being arrested but it will cost some people everything.

That marker, driven so early into the life of the church, is vitally important. Death goes hand in hand with growth. Given the order of events in Acts, we are taught that martyrdom might not simply be the consequence of growth, it might be the means by which God builds his church. After all, Christ won through the cross. Do we think that the growth of the church is going to be nothing but excitement and religious fun? If the church is to grow, there will be seed sown in tears and blood. The blood of the martyrs really is the seed of the church. Currently we experience almost nothing of this in the United Kingdom; but in many parts of the world it is the norm. Wherever we are placed, being a fellow-builder is no game. It is a joyous and serious business that God is about in this evil world.

Another point is being made for us with respect to our own normal Christian living: those who live well die well. It seems that in the seizing and the stoning of Stephen there is a direct connection between living well and dying well. Imprisoned in Rome and facing the prospect of martyrdom, Paul writes to the church in Philippi. He reflects on the alternatives that a trial and, probably, his execution will present to him. 'I eagerly expect and hope that I will in no way be ashamed, but will have sufficient courage so that now as always Christ will be exalted in my body, whether by life or by death' (Phil. 1:20). Staggering, really, when we think of it: the highest One in heaven and earth, with the greatest name in the universe, who wields all power and authority and who is enthroned in glory, can be made greater ('magnified' is the Greek word behind the English word 'exalted') by what I do in and with this body. We cannot, nay must not, develop some kind of austere mentality that looks down on the physical life. Despite the cultural preoccupation with enhancing this life, something about how we will die should become part of our understanding of what it means to live as God's fellow-builders. We live well – to the glory of God – and we die well; so that whether by living or dying, Christ is exalted in our bodies. Stephen died well because his dying was part and parcel of the way that he had lived. He wasn't catapulted into heroic martyrdom, having been a spiritual zero up until then.

Stephen

Luke gives us Stephen's story in three parts: he is seized, then he speaks, then he is stoned to death. But before Luke tells us about the arrest, he tells us about the man.

His character and his actions

A crisis has hit the church. Many of the believers are poor, especially the widows who, without their husbands, would have little or no source of income and relied entirely on the kindness of others. The love of Christ prompts members of the new family that these widows have been brought into the church to supply their needs. Great idea, great motive, but it's not working. The distribution is riddled with favouritism and spiritual elitism. In the church in Jerusalem there are converted Greek Jews and converted Hebrew Jews. The first group's native tongue is not the 'language of Zion', Hebrew (or more likely, the variant of it called Aramaic). The Greek speakers use the foreign tongue learned by Jews since the first dispersal centuries before, the tongue of the empire that produced so much bitterness in the Jews. So, in a process of blatant discrimination, the widows in the Hebrew-speaking group receive kindness while the Greek-speaking widows get nothing.

The apostles gather together the increasing number of disciples (at this time the only title used – no-one has coined the title 'Christians' yet) and make a proposal to improve the distribution. Put the food into the hands of a reasonable number of men who are trustworthy and Spirit-filled. Let the apostles get on with their God-given priorities and let the distribution of food be done in a way that pleases God. The proposal of the Twelve pleases the whole group.

Stephen's character was full of virtue. We notice first of all in Acts 6:3 that the Twelve said, 'Brothers, choose seven men from among you who are known to be full of the Spirit and wisdom.' Then in verse 5, 'They chose Stephen, a man full of faith and of the Holy Spirit.' Add in verse 8, 'Now Stephen, a man full of God's grace and power. . .'

So many things fill our lives. We juggle activities, but we also do an inner juggling act with the emotions and ambitions, the character traits and motives that are piled up within. What are you full of? Are you full of guilt and does that motivate you? Are you full of worries and anxieties? Are you full of bitterness? It can take root so easily in a Christian's life and grow through the years to make you bitter on the inside – and it shows. Are you full of the world and all its bright, dazzling desires and baubles? Are you full of love for a person, or a possession, or a habit, or a place, which has displaced your love for Christ? What are you full of? Are you full of the Spirit and wisdom, full of faith, full of God's grace and God's power?

I find it immensely challenging that Stephen is not an apostle, not one of the Twelve. He is just a man in the church, and yet he is so full of such gifts and graces that when Luke wants to talk about Stephen he finds himself describing Christ. Stephen is full of the Spirit. Jesus was full of the Holy Spirit (Lk. 4:1). Stephen is full of wisdom. What does Isaiah say of Jesus? 'The Spirit of the Lord will rest on him – the Spirit of wisdom and of understanding' (11:2). Stephen is full of grace. In John 1:14 we read of Jesus, 'The Word became flesh and made his dwelling among us. We have seen his glory, the glory of the One and Only, who came from the Father, full of grace and truth.' Stephen is full of power. The whole of Isaiah 11:2 goes on to describe the one who will come as having 'the Spirit of counsel and of power'.

Stephen is so full of the life of God that he gets described in the ways in which the Son of God is described. 'Now Stephen, a man full of God's grace and power, did great wonders and miraculous signs among the people' (verse 8).

He isn't just Christ-like in his character, but he is Christ-like in his deeds. God does through Stephen those things which he had also done through Christ. Even though Stephen is not one of the apostles, he is repeating the pattern laid down by Christ. We will see more of this as the story goes on. We noted it in Peter's life but it is significant here because it is a pattern that is found in the life of one of the 'ordinary' believers. Challenging, but also heartening.

Jesus said 'You will do greater things than these.' After he had gone to the Father and sent the Spirit, there would be so many more people doing God's works in so many more places. Jesus was in one place at one time, but the church grew quickly after his return to the Father and it will spread yet further until these things happen all over the world, after the pattern of Jesus.

Stephen becomes part of this growth as responsibility is laid upon him. He and the other six in this group, together with the Twelve, caused the church to grow as the work was shared. It is one of the dynamics of a growing church that it doesn't need fewer people who have been gifted, trained, resourced and set apart for their work, it actually needs more. If you want to promote growth you don't trim down the number of what in the past have been called 'clergy' or, less quaintly, 'full-time Christian workers' (the most recent attempt seems to be 'salaried Christians' – Lovely? Not!) On the contrary, if you want to engage the giftedness of the whole body of believers to exercise God-given ministries you need more people who, quite simply, have the time to develop areas of the church's life in which the ministry of the rest of the folk can flourish. People are freed up to shoulder extra responsibilities and are given the time to step back from the ordinary stuff of life to think and pray and discern strategies that would be helpful.

You've only got twenty-four hours in a day, and if you've got a normal job to do you've only got so much time and energy left to give to other activities: shopping, ferrying the kids around, seeing friends and family, eating and if you're fortunate, sleeping. Add to that the needs of the fellowship and your desire to see it thrive. Then spice it all up with a dash of the guilt that many of us in leadership seem to be good at inducing ('We need more *commitment*, people – what are your priorities? Don't you *care* about the lost and don't you *love* the Lord?') It's the perfect recipe for individual and corporate exhaustion and frustration. The problems of elitism and the proliferation of management are serious, but setting apart good leadership encourages growth, as it did there in Jerusalem.

Notice that Stephen not only has a Christ-like character, and does Christ-like deeds; he also becomes a very vocal witness to Christ: he speaks. The Spirit in him not only enables him to do miraculous wonders and signs among the people but the Spirit in him also bears verbal witness. Again, it is just part of what the Spirit does to repattern the character of Christ in the life of the believers. The Spirit is described as another Comforter, that is, one just like Christ. Living in us, he reproduces in us what Christ was doing. As Christ spoke, so now those who are filled with the Spirit speak. It is just a little reminder to us that if we want more of the Spirit of God (or if we want the Spirit of God to have more of us, which is probably more of a challenge) then he will use us to speak. We will become mouthpieces for the word of God in one way or another.

Stephen is able to articulate his faith and debate with a cool head in the heat of spiritual battle. He has irresistible wisdom because he has the Spirit of God in him. We read in Acts 6:10 that men from the synagogue began to argue with Stephen, but they could not stand up against his wisdom or the Spirit by whom he spoke. He has suddenly become a lot cleverer. He can pull quotes in from all over the Old Testament; he can build an argument and, as Peter had done, nail the opposition. But that blessing of irresistible wisdom is precisely what's going to get him into so much trouble. Again, if we want blessings from God, we had better be prepared for the consequences.

The Opposition

Stephen stirs up animosity quickly. It starts in the Synagogue of the Freedmen. The Roman Emperor Pompey had captured many Jews from all over the empire and then released them in Rome in 63 BC to show just how generous he was. Many of them had gone back to Jerusalem, and their descendants, along with those of others whom Pompey had freed, would have been in

Jerusalem to join their fellow-countrymen for the feast of the Passover. Those from the freed families still held their own worship in, possibly, several of their own synagogues.

Like Stephen, they are Greek-speaking Jews. Unlike Stephen, they are intensely loyal to their Judaism and intensely angry at what Stephen stands for. But they cannot win. Rendered ineffective by the wisdom of Stephen and the Spirit of God, they persuade some men to say, 'We have heard Stephen speak words of blasphemy against Moses and against God' (Acts 6:11). In so doing, they stir up quite a crowd; the people, the elders and the teachers of the law. The whole mob then drags them before the power brokers, the Sanhedrin.

It's a cleverly put together arrangement. Notice the players. Stirring up the people on their own wouldn't work because there was a fear in Jerusalem of stirring up a crowd. The Romans clamped down harshly on public disorder and everybody suffered. But if you could stir up the elders then you are doing better: you've got some of the leaders of Israel's noble families, some of whom were members of the Sanhedrin. If you can also stir up the teachers of the law, then you've really got the whole Jewish establishment on your side. How instructive that, in the name of the religion of the God who gave the Ten Commandments, the one concerning false witness against your neighbour is ignored lest it get in the way of personal power and entrenched resistance to Christ. Those who profess to worship him, and who are so defensive about their worship of him, are in fact full of evil antagonism towards God, and express it here in hatred of his fellow-builder, Stephen.

Once again, the Sanhedrin have a Christian in front of them. This one doesn't back down either. What is going on here? To see just how momentous an event this is, we need to step back from the immediate action and take in the bigger picture: what is going on between Christ's first coming and his second coming? It is a clash of empires, of cities and spiritual powers. It is a huge, constant struggle. In the terms that we read in the book of Revelation, there is a city that is in rebellion against God, variously called Sodom, Egypt or, most memorably, Babylon. The city represents the kingdom of this world in its rebellion against God. Wherever the gospel is sounded out clearly, by life, by deed and by word, then that kingdom is going to oppose it.

So the question that arises is not 'Why are we Christians so comfortable with the world?' but the reverse: 'Why is the world so comfortable with us?' The world should not be comfortable with us. By our characters, our actions and our speech, we are constantly threatening the power in this world. We should be a constant threat to people's security outside of God. We should be a constant threat to the strengthening of sin in this world. Stephen posed such a threat to the Sanhedrin that they couldn't be comfortable for very long while Stephen was around.

So why is the world so comfortable with the church? I mean the non-Christians where we live? It's not that we want to make our colleagues squirm, or make our relatives miserable; it's not that we want our neighbours to dislike us. It is that we want them to come to Christ because in some way they become uncomfortable with where they are in relation to God.

The approach to preaching the gospel which says that we affirm people 'where they are' has no foundation in a biblical understanding of the gospel. We might affirm them as human beings by valuing their lives and eternal destiny more than they do, but what we never read happening in Jerusalem and then Judea, Samaria and to the uttermost parts of the world, and what we never read happening in Revelation, is that the gospel affirms sinners 'where they are'. *God* does not affirm people where they are. They are dead in their transgressions and sins. God meets people where they are because, loving them, he doesn't want them to remain there; he's going to move them somewhere better. The world should be uncomfortable with us and it might, in that discomfort, seek the Christ whom we proclaim. It might also, in that discomfort, hate him and so hate us. Either way, we will not have colluded in the great deception that the norm is normal.

It is this greater struggle between the two powers, the two cities, which erupts here. Like Satan in Revelation 12, the Freedmen were bad losers. They began to argue with Stephen and they lost. Their pride was wounded. It must be very humiliating to pick a fight in public and lose.

I was once on the sea-front at Llandudno in North Wales, on a beach mission. It was Saturday, the day when new teams arrive. We quickly put a singing group together and mercilessly launched our music upon innocent holidaymakers. Having thus attracted a crowd, one of the leaders called up a team member to give their testimony. One of the girls stood on the box and was 'cross-questioned' about how she became a Christian. A well-educated man in the crowd started heckling. He attacked the girl over the authorship of John's Gospel. (Such was the level of public debate of a Saturday night in North Wales at the time!) He lost. Partly he lost because a number of the blokes in the crowd became protective of the girl in a male sort of a way. But the team-leader who was interviewing the girl also 'knew his stuff'. He answered the heckler point for point and basically beat him with better scholarship. After only a few minutes, the heckler lost more than the argument: he lost face in front of his sons and he lost his composure, becoming increasingly bad-tempered and abusive.

The Freedmen were bad losers who were zealous, numerous and connected with the Sanhedrin. And in their own estimation, they had a lot to lose. With their pride wounded, they became enraged. On the one hand, we see God's fellow-builder Stephen, full of grace and power, full of wisdom, full of the Spirit. On the other, we see the opposers of the kingdom, full of pride and bitterness and getting worse.

The opposition came because Stephen wounded their sacred cows; Moses and the Temple. 'This fellow never stops speaking against this holy place and against the law. For we have heard him say that this Jesus of Nazareth will destroy this place and change the customs Moses handed down to us' (Acts 6:13,14).

The preaching of the apostles and the arguments of Stephen attacked the core of their false religion. Stephen has hit their idols hard with the truth of the gospel. If we do the same then we can expect a rough ride. It doesn't matter if the sacred cow is the church denomination, or lack of it. It doesn't matter if the sacred cow is promiscuity or perversion, low-life drunkenness or high-minded relativism. It doesn't matter what it is: when sacred cows are stabbed it causes uproar.

Why? Because a person's god is their glory, the best thing about them. When the gospel confronts a person's god it threatens them as people because it threatens the best thing they've got in their life. It attacks what they live for, what they are devoted to, what they trust. The gospel attacks, subtly or otherwise, their reason for being here. That god might be wealth, or sport, or sex. It might be health and fitness, or their religion or their career – it doesn't really matter what it is. The gospel proclaims the one true God who is against any false god, who said 'I am the LORD; that is my name! I will not give my glory to another or my praise to idols' (Is. 42:8). Stephen, in Jerusalem then, did what the gospel does in our own places now. From Chipping Camden to Calcutta, from Donegal to Dar-es-Salaam, from Baltimore to Bangkok, the message that the God and father of our Lord Jesus Christ is the one true and living God exposes idolatry.

Do we not also see that behind the Synagogue of the Freedmen is the power-base referred to in the letters to the seven churches in Revelation, the synagogue of Satan? Do we not see the hand of God's enemy reaching out through the Synagogue of the Freedmen to kill the church as it had tried to kill the Saviour?

But of course, though it killed Christ, it lost. And though it kills his fellow-builder, it's going to lose again.

In the Midst of the Storm

What about Stephen? What about the man in the midst of the storm?

He shows amazing courage. As the storm of rage and malice worsens, his bravery only grows. But this is how God works in his servants' lives. Why doesn't Stephen back down? He has the opportunity to do so and could justify it any number of ways. He could save the rest of the fellowship any antagonism; he could avert an unseemly disturbance that might reflect badly on the name of Jesus; he could bow out and return to what was, after all, his real role of serving food. But he doesn't back down. He keeps his head above the parapet.

He shows an unshakable allegiance to the truth and an immovable commitment to Christ. Jesus and his gospel mean more to Stephen than his own life. They captivate him more than safe Christian service does. Remember the slogan on the back of the shirt of that OM worker: 'The ship is safe and comfortable in the harbour. But that's not what ships are for.' Stephen does not use quiet, in-house Christian service as a bolt-hole.

His wisdom rises to meet the danger. Spirit-filled, he shows the ability to speak as well as the nerve to stand his ground and say what needed to be said whatever the cost. What Jesus promised in Luke 12:11,12 is exactly what happens, detail for detail, in Stephen's life: 'When you are brought before synagogues, rulers and authorities, do not worry about how you will defend yourselves or what you will say, for the Holy Spirit will teach you at that time what you should say.'

Again, Luke 21:10 to 15:

> Then he said to them: 'Nation will rise against nation, and kingdom against kingdom. There will be great earthquakes, famines and pestilences in various places, and fearful events and great signs from heaven. But before all this, they will lay hands on you and persecute you. They will deliver you to synagogues and prisons, and you will be brought before kings and governors, and all on account of my name. This will result in your being witnesses to them. But make up your mind not to worry beforehand how you will defend yourselves. For I will give you words and wisdom that none of your adversaries will be able to resist or contradict.'

As promised and by the Spirit with whom he is filled, Stephen receives the resources for the moment.

God still does this for us, even though we wrack ourselves with worry as if he did not care. That is *not* to say that if we are given advance notice that we'll have to speak about Jesus we should never prepare. A German pastor tells how a younger pastor, Heinrich, was on his way out of the pulpit after having preached. He boasted to the older pastor that he hadn't wasted time preparing the sermon, instead he had trusted the Spirit to speak to him and tell him what to say. The older pastor said, 'Well, the Spirit spoke to me also. The Spirit gave me three words: "Heinrich, you're lazy!"' Stephen is not lazy; he's not in that kind of situation. This is a situation of persecution with the potential for being silenced by fear. In precisely this kind of situation, 'Do not worry how you will defend yourself.' This is a situation where his words will determine whether he will live or die. In that situation, worrying beforehand does no good. How will you know that you're going to say the right thing? You could plan and prepare. You could have a dozen speeches up a dozen sleeves and your fear would still rob you of your words. God gives Stephen all that he needs for the moment to which he has brought him.

But God gave something else to Stephen because, it would seem from the story, Stephen was looking somewhere else. Verse 15: 'All who were sitting in the Sanhedrin looked intently at Stephen (if looks could kill!) and they saw that his face was like the face of an angel.'

Stephen was looking up. We will read in the next chapter of Acts that when the mob rush at him to stone him 'Stephen, full of the Holy Spirit, looked up to heaven and saw the glory of God.' I think that back here at the start of the trial, when maybe he had some inkling of what was coming, though we don't know, he has looked up, and God is looking down on him. God has given him the 'countenance of heaven'. Whatever it was, it must have had the most amazing effect upon those who were there. Especially since these people had turned Moses into one of their gods. Read this, from Adam Clarke's old commentary on Acts:

It appears that the light and power of God which dwelt in his soul shone through his face and God gave them this proof of the falsity of the testimony which was now before them, for as the face of Stephen now shone as the face of Moses did when he came down from the mount, it was the fullest proof that he had not spoken blasphemous words either against Moses or God, else this splendour of Heaven had not rested upon him. The history of the apostolic church is a series of wonders. Everything that could prevent such a church from being established or could overthrow it when established is brought to bear against it. The instruments employed in its building and defence had neither might nor power but what came immediately from God.[1]

Those who had accused Stephen of blasphemy against Moses and against God see on Stephen's face the vindication of God upon his man. Never forget the power of God to speak through the look on your face.

The Emerging Pattern

The pattern repeats itself

The story of what God did in his fellow-builders' lives constantly reveals the pattern of Christ's life. As the Father and the Spirit supplied all that the Son needed, so now, together with the Son, they meet Stephen's great need. God had revealed himself as the provider-king, Jehovah-Jireh, in the Old Testament; now Stephen experiences that sovereign provision for himself. But God promises this for all his fellow-workers – including you and me now: 'God will meet all your needs according to his glorious riches in Christ Jesus' (Phil. 4:19). It need never be doubted, for the promise is not a statement about our faith. It does not say 'your faith will supply all your needs'. It does not even say that he will meet all our needs according to the enormity or otherwise of our faith. We think like this: if we really concentrate extra specially hard so that our brows become furrowed, God will see our earnest faith and will provide according to that earnestness. Or perhaps we feel that if we mention a need with a kind of throwaway casualness, as if our faith was so big that we hardly need mention to God the thing that actually we can't stop worrying about – the lump, the overdraft, the son who has been doing drugs – then God will be so impressed by our supposedly easy assumption that it's no problem to him, that he's bound to provide. No, Philippians 4:19 is a statement about God: the promise to you is that your needs will be met by him according to his glorious riches – according to the size of God's storehouse, not the 'size' of your faith.

Catch the humour in the way that Jesus debunks the 'size of your faith' myth in Matthew 17:20. He paints the delightfully memorable picture – memorable because of his deliberate use of a teaching technique that we could call 'hilarious absurdity' – of the 'size' of faith needed to do large-scale landscaping: faith as tiny as a mustard seed can fling mountains around. The point is that 'size' isn't the point – it's the One believed in who's important. What the Father did for his Son, the true Builder, and what he was doing here for Stephen, he does for all those who build with him; it's the same God on the same mission.

Next, we need to look at Stephen's speech and see how he handles the word of truth, which is the tool of the kingdom-builder's trade.

To ponder

- Are you afraid of what people might think of you if you spoke about Jesus? If so, can you bring that fear to God now – he's immensely understanding? Can you ask for courage, or would you rather hang on to the fear since it can work as an excuse to blend in with your surroundings, like a chameleon?
- What if God doesn't have a quiet life in store for you – what might be the benefits to his mission of you not having a quiet life? Can you let go of the predictability of your days? Can you let go of your fear of failure?
- How can you be bold without being arrogant, or a pain in the neck of every non-Christian that you meet?
- Do the people around you believe in something called 'truth'? If so, does it have any connection with anything or anyone that they might call 'God'?

Chapter 5

Courageously Speaking the Truth

Stephen's Speech

'Preach the Word; be prepared in season and out of season' (2 Tim. 4:2).

Stephen's speech occupies most of Acts chapter 7. Work with me here: we need to dig into it for a while, unearthing the Old Testament background, teasing out details, reading with our eyes peeled. The sense of it might be a bit blurred at first, but when it comes into focus, we see one perfectly aimed shaft of truth that ends in as sharp a point as we will find anywhere in the Bible. We also see that it hits the target. To understand what Stephen is doing here is worth the effort. To see what God is doing makes it even more worthwhile, for aspects of this chapter show us more of what we should expect God to do with us so that we might become better builders. In addition, it might just blow your socks off!

Setting the scene

Stephen's experience takes a parallel track to Christ's: 'doctrinal' conflict, hatred, manipulation of the legal system, death. Following Jesus means exactly that: going where he's gone. It is costly, but ultimately it is glorious. The verb for 'witness' in the Greek is the word *marturio*, from which we derive the word 'martyr'. Witness and martyrdom were inseparable in the language of the early church; a martyr was simply a witness whose witnessing cost them their life. To be called and empowered for witnessing is to be called and empowered even for death; but beyond death lies glory.

Stephen is in the grip of the Sanhedrin, having been seized by men from the Synagogue of the Freedmen. Their disgust at the miracles and their offence at the preaching have now taken a strategic turn – no longer is it mere hatred, now it's hatred with a plan; and the plan is being given legal support via the Sanhedrin.

To strengthen their case they have wheeled in false witnesses – ironic that a witness to the truth should be discredited by false witnesses. It's the way of the world to prefer lies if they shield sin from the searchlight of God's truth. The claim, in Acts 6:11, is that Stephen has been speaking words of blasphemy against Moses, against God, and against the Temple. 'Moses' doesn't just mean Moses personally, though as we'll see, the people had turned him into an icon, not to say an idol. 'Moses' (as verse 13 shows) stands for the first five books of the Old Testament, 'the Law', particularly the Ten Commandments in Exodus 20 and the regulations that follow. But 'the Law' also included the laws and customs that had been added to God's word over the years by the scribes, additions that were regarded as having the same authority as the Scriptures.

The moment could not be more highly charged. Power surges and crackles between two spiritual kingdoms; the current finds earth in the fate of this one man. Suddenly, with no time to prepare a carefully thought-out strategy or a finely crafted sermon, Stephen and the church are catapulted into this defining moment. We don't get to witness when *we think* we ought to; we witness when *he knows* that the building of his kingdom requires it.

Think of some of the possibilities for just a few seconds. What will Stephen say? Will he back down? Will he fudge the issues? Will he try and pacify the mob and protect himself? Will he deny Christ? No-one there has the rest of Acts to refer to: they don't know how the next few moments, let alone the next few years, will turn out. As yet, the church has not faced the kind of fury and madness that now gather, storm-like, around Stephen. What will be the character of the church? Will it tailor the message to preserve an easy life? Will the church carry the radical power of new life, or will it bow to the old? Will it pay the earthly price for obedience to heaven? Will it take part in the building of God's house or will it shore up the world's houses? When push comes to more than shove, which kingdom will it belong to?

These are precisely the questions that face the church today. In many parts of the world they are brought into the open by obvious persecution. In many other places – the affluent and sophisticated West, for instance – they are less clear, obscured by that fact that we can get on with an apparently normal life without being tortured or having our churches bombed. But the possibilities are still the same.

The battle commences. The high priests ask Stephen, 'Are these charges true?' Stephen's explosive and devastating reply runs from Acts 7:1 to 53.

Before the particulars, notice this first, general point: Stephen preaches as Christ had preached. It's a vital lesson for our own handling of the Bible in any situation, not just traditional preaching. When the Spirit takes what is Christ's and makes it ours, he will teach us about

Christ, and he will also reproduce the character and the ways of Christ in us. As Stephen preaches, not just with words but also with power, with the Spirit and with deep conviction (to anticipate the description that Paul gives of the way in which he preached in Thessalonica) it becomes more than a sermon *about* Christ: it becomes a Christ-*like* sermon. This likeness honours Christ and is glorifying to God.

Stephen's preaching is like Christ's in three ways.

First, Jesus repeatedly made the same basic point that Stephen has to make here: you've got Moses all wrong: you've turned the whole thing upside down in order to suit yourselves. Jesus made the point, for instance, in the Sermon on the Mount, 'You have heard it said, but I say to you.' 'You have heard it said' referred to the teaching of the rabbis and scribes who twisted Moses' law and the rules and regulations that surrounded it to suit the sinfulness of the people. So they reshaped the law on, for instance, divorce in such a way that you could divorce your wife if you got the paperwork right. That was the only thing you needed. They completely inverted what God had given for the protection of society and families in general and women in particular; they put a self-serving veneer on the law. Jesus constantly stripped back that veneer in order to uncover the truth.

Second, Stephen raises the question of discipleship, another recurring theme in the challenge that Jesus issued. The Jewish leaders venerated Moses as God's leader in the rescue from Egypt, the great model for understanding God's saving work. And he was revered as the law-giving prophet who spoke the very words of God. But he was only a man. Despite their elevation of Moses, he was only a servant of God. Yet 'blasphemy' is the charge levelled against Stephen. Since when did you blaspheme against a man? The words that Moses had spoken, as well as some that he hadn't, meant so much to the scribes that the man became inseparable from the words. It's a kind of idolatry; it can still happen among those who highly value the word of God and love good Bible teaching. Love the teaching; slip into idolising the teacher.

If we turn back the pages to John 9:28, we see Jesus facing the same thing. We read of a man who was born blind and whom Jesus had just healed. He is being grilled by the Pharisees, who really don't like people getting healed by Jesus. It is way too messianic a sign, and might lend credibility to the obviously blasphemous claim that Jesus really is the Messiah.

> Then they asked him, 'What did he do to you? How did he open your eyes?' He answered, 'I have told you already and you did not listen. Why do you want to hear it again? Do you want to become his disciples, too?' Then they hurled insults at him and said, 'You are this fellow's disciple! We are disciples of Moses! . . . We know that God spoke to Moses, but as for this fellow, we don't even know where he comes from' (Jn. 9:26ff).

There's the tension: two Lords, two masters to follow. They had made their choice: rejecting the conclusion that Jesus really is the Messiah, really is God among them, they follow Moses. If you're not a disciple of Jesus Christ, you're going to be a disciple of somebody else.

Thus the false witnesses, choosing an accusation that they know will incriminate Stephen, say, 'This fellow never stops speaking against this holy place and against the law. For we have heard him say that this Jesus of Nazareth will destroy this place and change the customs Moses handed down to us' (Acts 6:13,14). Like the

Master-builder, Stephen has come up against determined opposition that focuses on who to follow, on who will be Lord. Stephen is treated badly because he chose Jesus.

Thirdly, Jesus repeatedly had to show that 'Moses points to me.' If we turn back to John 5, we see a pointed summary of what Jesus has just been teaching: 'But do not think that I will accuse you before the Father. Your accuser is Moses, on whom your hopes are set. If you believed Moses, you would believe me, for he wrote about me' (Jn. 5:45,46).

Stephen picks up exactly the same point in Acts 7:37. Moses had written about Jesus in Deuteronomy 18:15, 'God will send you a prophet like me from your own people.' The blinkered vision of the teachers of the law and the Pharisees meant that they didn't believe Jesus, and they didn't believe Moses either. In John 5, Jesus goes on to say, 'But since you do not believe what he wrote, how are you going to believe what I say?' (verse 47).

As Stephen makes the point that they don't even believe Moses, he strips away their religious falsity and hypocrisy. He uncovers the truth of those Scriptures that the teachers of the law claimed to understand but in fact rejected. Their hearts and minds were so far from God that they could pick over each letter of the law and even teach it to the nation, yet never see that it pointed to Jesus. Of all the people who were around at the time, the people now trying Stephen were the ones who should have most welcomed and worshipped the Messiah, in whose name Stephen acted and spoke. They didn't just get Moses wrong, they rejected the One to whom Moses pointed.

The History Lesson: You Have Always Rejected God's Men

Here we begin to engage with the flow of the argument a little more closely. Stephen gives them a history lesson. That's audacious in the company he is in: these men are the gatekeepers of history. They control not only the 'facts' but also how to read them: they enforce the truth regime. Stephen is going to demolish their intellectual and spiritual property and attack the foundations of their empire.

He begins by mentioning Abraham. Why? Well, at one level, Stephen points to the fact that although they claim that Abraham is their spiritual father, their hearts betray that they are not his sons. But by starting with Abraham he is also signalling the way in which God deals with his people to bless them: according to his promises, not their goodness. God's promise to Abraham of land is followed by the promise of children. In the context of these promises comes a mention of the covenant sign of circumcision. It is the sign of Abraham's acceptance by faith of God's gifts; a sign of his trust in the God who deals promises from the deck of grace.

Joseph was rejected

Then he moves on to Joseph, through whom the line of promise continued and yet who was rejected. This is where the stripping away of the Sanhedrin's falsity begins. Stephen points out that Joseph, whom God had set his hand upon, was rejected by his circumcised brothers. They were of the same family and in their flesh they had the same sign of faith in God, yet they of all people had set their hearts against God's man. So, 'Because the patriarchs were jealous of Joseph, they sold him as a slave into Egypt. But God was with him' (Acts 7:9).

Brilliantly, Stephen has flagged up opposition to *the*
promised One, Jesus. See how he spells it out, each point
laced with bitter challenge for those in front of him. What
sets the patriarchs against Joseph is jealousy-inspired
hatred. He'd got something that they didn't have and
they hated him for it. Why does Stephen say that to the
Sanhedrin? Because he wants them to see that jealous
people, with hatred in their hearts yet who were circumcised and who appeared to be of the same family as
Joseph, rejected him. But also he wants them to see that
God was with Joseph, and God vindicated his man.
Those who had rejected him ended up having to come to
him for life and bow to him. (There were, by the way,
roughly seventy men in the Sanhedrin listening to
Stephen. Stephen unsubtly points out to them that there
were seventy-five who had to go and shelter under
Joseph's care. Spot the connection!) Events laid bare the
desperately suppressed truth that Joseph *was* God's man.

In passing, notice this: as Stephen speaks of Joseph's
saving provision he introduces 'saving grace'. The
brothers sold him. But then they faced death through
starvation. By providing food for them, Joseph saved
those who had tried to eliminate him and reconciled the
family under their father Jacob.

Moses was rejected

'Then another king, who knew nothing about Joseph,
became ruler of Egypt. He dealt treacherously with our
people and oppressed our fathers by forcing them to
throw out their newborn babies so that they would die.
At that time Moses was born and he was no ordinary
child' (Acts 7:18-20). As with Joseph, so with Moses. He
was rejected repeatedly (from the heart) by his own
people, by those who were circumcised on the outside,

those who belonged to the same nation and who were heirs of the same promise. So, 'But the man who was ill-treating the other pushed Moses aside and said, "Who made you ruler and judge over us? Do you want to kill me as you killed the Egyptian yesterday?" When Moses heard this, he fled to Midian, where he settled as a foreigner and had two sons' (Acts 7:27–29).

'You made him an outcast. People just like you, people who were of the same spiritual kingdom as you rejected him then,' he declares. Not, it has to be said, the usual point that we hear being made from this episode in Moses' life. Normally it's 'Don't take God's work into your own hands, at your own time, according to your own temper. Carve for yourself and you'll cut your own fingers. You need schooling in obedience first. Maybe for forty years.' (At which point those in their sixties gulp.)

As far as Spirit-filled Stephen is concerned, however, it was the fellow-Hebrews who were at fault, not Moses. It makes sense: isn't it more than a bit perverse to react so bitterly against one who so forcefully identifies with you? Moses acted from the depths of his own heart and at such cost to himself, in order to take up their cause. Bit like Christ, come to think of it. I mean, whose side were these Hebrews on? The slave-master's? Did they prefer oppression by Pharaoh to rescue by Moses? It makes you think. It made the Sanhedrin think.

Stephen hits them again. 'This is the same Moses whom they had rejected with the words, "Who made you ruler and judge?" He was sent to be their . . .' (Stop! Wait a moment before you read on. Are we tuned in to where Stephen is taking this sermon? These words have almost incalculable significance. Are we going to hear whom he is really talking about?) 'He was sent to be their ruler and deliverer by God himself.' Of whom do those words speak? Without using his name, Stephen is already speaking about Jesus. The sub-text says '*Jesus* was sent to be *your* ruler and deliverer by God himself, by the One whom you profess to worship, about whom you claim to be experts and whose work you like to think you're doing.' Which makes verse 39 particularly barbed: 'But our fathers refused to obey him. Instead, they rejected him and in their hearts turned back to Egypt.'

The rejection continued at Sinai. The Israelites were present with Moses physically, but in their hearts they were back in the land whence they came. Quick to forget the harsh realities of their lives under Pharaoh's slave-drivers, they longed for the juicy niceties. With hearts like that, small wonder they didn't obey Moses. No wonder they made a calf and worshipped it. They told Aaron, 'Make us gods who will go before us.' No wonder they became (and are we listening again as Stephen is preaching it?) idolaters. No wonder they worshipped someone or something other than God.

Do we see what he accuses them of having done with Jesus? Pick the argument up from the references to Joseph. 'His brothers rejected him. You men of the synagogue are Joseph's brothers. They ended up having to bow to him. You will have to do the same with the One that you've rejected. Joseph saved them. Jesus would save you if you came to him.' Then see how Stephen's line of argument continues with reference to Moses. 'Moses was the deliverer and the ruler whom God had sent. In their hearts his own people rejected him and worshipped something that they had made, something of their own concoction. This is the pattern that you are repeating, but this time you are doing it with God's own Son. You have rejected the Son in favour of your religious idol.'

The tabernacle of the Testimony was rejected

This is a wonderful way of describing the tent that was the moveable meeting place between God and man through the wilderness and into the Promised Land.

'Our forefathers had the tabernacle of the Testimony with them in the desert. It had been made as God directed Moses, according to the pattern he had seen. Having received the tabernacle, our fathers under Joshua brought it with them when they took the land from the nations God drove out before them. It remained in the land until the time of David, who enjoyed God's favour' (Acts 7:44–46).

Stephen piles on another example of something from God that was rejected by the people. Stephen speaks about David here: a brave thing to do when you're facing this body of people some of whom would love to see Davidic rule re-established. David enjoyed God's favour, looking ahead to an everlasting Ruler who would sit on his throne; yet even David rejected what God had directed him to do. He preferred to replace the God-designed tabernacle of the testimony with a building that he would design.

Notice what Stephen is driving at. God sent the pattern for the tent. It came down from him. When the tabernacle was built it was what God wanted and it was the way God wanted it. But even a man who enjoyed God's favour could reject God's revealed will. The point? You enjoy God's favour but you've rejected the One God sent. You've rejected his appointed meeting place between himself and sinful humanity. You've constructed your own religious edifice. You haven't accepted God's building plan. Instead you've decided to build something for God.

He is telling the Sanhedrin, in extremely pointed language, that they are the very opposite of God's fellow-builders. God said, 'Build a tabernacle and build it this way' but they had revered a Temple that mere men (Herod, by this time) had built to their own glory. Stephen is pointing out what it means to be the very opposite of one of God's fellow-builders: to replace what God has sent down and revealed as his will with something that you want to do for him in order to admire yourselves. Instead of being a fellow-builder with God, as those who built the tabernacle were, you become the builder. You construct a way to meet with God and you have the audacity to assume that God is so pleased with it that he's going to swing down and co-operate with you.

The point is as sharply relevant now as it was then. Even a man after God's own heart like David could get it really wrong by wanting to build his own edifice for God. If he could, so can we; so can the church in the West, or the growing church in Eastern Europe or China. The temptation to try to build God's church for him in order to impress him or to earn distinction within the Christian community is a strong one for any in leadership. Equally, the ability of Christians to pressurise the leaders into listening to them rather than to God, has to be recognised as a hindrance to the growth of the church. Leaders who think 'I want it my way' and congregations who want it their way both act out of the same pride and suffer from the same religious conceit. The mentality produces a way of doing church that creates celebrities out of leaders, that successfully competes in the church marketplace, and that builds a monument to human religious achievement. The plans, the skills, the tools and gauges of such false building work are well-known. We go for size: either big must be good, or small must mean really 'sound and serious'. We go for wealth: either loving it or staying self-righteously untainted by it. We fall in love with preachers who ooze success, look good enough for TV, and in whose polished sentences we can admire our own choice of church. Or we build a church that becomes a kind of statue to a dead leader. His style and teaching become our yardsticks and spirit-levels. We read what he read, sing what he liked and despise whatever he denounced. But who do mega-churches tend to make famous? Who do small fellowships, that hang on to the memory of their founders and that go down in history with them, tend to honour most? For whom do we build?

David, whom God loved, got it wrong; so had the people represented by the Sanhedrin, whom God also loved. They too, had rejected the One whom God had sent, the One in whom God and man would meet. The tabernacle speaks of Christ. The writer of Hebrews said that it was an earthly copy of heavenly realities (Heb. 8:5). The reality is Christ. The tabernacle functions as a type of Christ and what David did with the tabernacle becomes a type of what they have done with God's Jesus. They have rejected the human tent where God and man will meet: Jesus Christ, in his flesh. They prefer something of their own devising instead. They are religious, but prefer *their* way of fellowship with God, not his. They have spurned the place where sin is going to be atoned for (Christ's body on the cross), preferring their own place of atonement (the altar in Herod's Temple in Jerusalem). They have rejected Jesus Christ as the One in whom God was at work reconciling the world to himself, preferring their own works.

You see how this sermon is going. It's stunning! No wonder that Luke described Stephen as being full of the Spirit and wisdom, full of faith and the Holy Spirit, full of God's grace and power. No wonder that the people of the

Synagogue of the Freedmen could not stand up against his wisdom or the Spirit by whom he spoke. This is the Spirit's awesome genius. I've tried to tease out these things, albeit haltingly and clumsily, in the hope that we see something of the perfect weight and balance with which the Spirit wields the double-bladed sword that he has put into the hands of his humble, courageous servant.

Stephen Follows Through: Now You've Rejected God

Bear with me. A perfectly pleasant-looking young man walks on to the set of Blue Peter and smashes through a pile of slate tiles with his bare hand: a frequent sight on children's TV in the late 1960s. Though I never tried it at home myself (I had friends who did) I gather that when you bring your hand down in such a karate chop, you don't aim at the tiles or even look at them. You aim at the floor, the tiles just happen to be in the way. As with karate, so with preaching, it's the follow-through that counts.

In a torrent of such blows, Stephen slices through their tough skin and follows through to the heart. 'You are just like your fathers.' The phrase 'your fathers' has biting irony in it. The language of the father/son relationship in their world refers not just to a biological connection, it's a way of saying that you take after someone. It's about being a chip off the old block. 'You're a son of thunder' doesn't mean 'Your parents had a stormy marriage' (though who knows . . .). It means 'You're just like thunder: you're noisy and unruly, you crash about and you're slightly exhilarating.'

So when Stephen says 'You are just like your fathers' he's not just meaning that the Sanhedrin were the genetic offspring of those who rejected God's men and God's ways in the past. He's saying, 'You *really do* show their likeness. They might be dead but we can see just what they were like when we look at you.' And in case the Sanhedrin has missed the particular family resemblance that Stephen has in mind, he gives them the diagnosis of their inherited condition: 'You are stiff-necked.' What a marvellous biblical phrase! 'You will not yield to God. You will not accept by faith that Jesus is God and that the most appropriate thing to do is to bow.' They show the same stubborn pride as their fathers showed.

The next blow strikes deeper. Their bodies might bear the mark of circumcision, the mark of accepting the promises of God's grace by faith, but in reality they have uncircumcised hearts and ears. Remember how in the past they rejected him 'in their hearts'? They are circumcised in the flesh, but on the inside they are unbelieving. There is no faith by which they depend on the promises of God. They merely have a religious way of trying to buy what God has promised to give. So they will not listen from the heart: they have uncircumcised hearts and ears. No faith in the hearing, just deafness in the heart. No submissiveness to the One who speaks to guide, convince and renew: 'You always resist the Holy Spirit!' (Acts 7:51).

He keeps up the barrage: 'Was there ever a prophet your fathers did not persecute? They even killed those who predicted the coming of the Righteous One' (verse 52). Though we don't come across the phrase 'the Righteous One' in the Gospels, it became an apostolic favourite. It belongs to those descriptions of God in the Old Testament.

Dig a little with me. Stephen picks out a title for Christ that establishes him as God's man among the Jews. It establishes him as what we might call the supreme Jew, since above all the pious Jew wanted to become righteous. It has an echo of Proverbs 21:12: 'The

Righteous One takes not of the house of the wicked and brings the wicked to ruin.' But the principal reference is to Isaiah 24:16: 'From the ends of the earth we hear singing: "Glory to the Righteous One." But I said, "I waste away, I waste away! Woe to me! The treacherous betray! With treachery the treacherous betray!"'

It's a devastatingly apt pick-up from the prophet. The context in Isaiah is that God has used the Assyrians as a rod of judgement to lay waste the whole of the Israelites' land. He has done so in righteous judgement – that is, it was the right thing for him to do, given his own holiness and his faithfulness to his own word. It was also the right thing for God to do because he is the saving God; he destroyed the land to save his people from the greater destruction that sin brings. How were the survivors of that destruction to react to the wrath of their God that had swept over their land – his land?

Two reactions find voice in the passage in Isaiah. The first sings a song of praise for the work of God. There are some who accept that what he has done is terrifyingly painful, but is right; and so they glorify and honour Jehovah the Righteous One. But there is a lone voice of dissent. This voice sees the wasteland and it cries 'Treachery!' God shouldn't have done this. If he is really our God he should have kept us free from the Assyrians. This lone complainer has seen none of the rightness of God. He has seen no need for repentance, no need for turning back to the One who had given warning after warning, and who in his holiness shows no partiality and no tolerance of sin. There is no sensitivity to the zeal of God for his own name and reputation. Many who long to proclaim mercy and grace to the guilty struggle over a God of wrath who judges people. Many have honest questions that trouble them deeply and that are untouched by trite clichés and pat answers. But all that this character can do is complain. In fact, all he shows toward God is exactly what he accuses God of: treachery.

Stephen's use of the title 'the Righteous One' evokes the picture of Jehovah's opposition to sin, even when he finds it in his own people; in fact especially when he finds it there. It refreshes the memory of a God who deals with sin neither by condoning it nor excusing it, but by purging it in order to save people from it. Stephen says that Jesus Christ is the Righteous One of whom Isaiah spoke. Jesus Christ is God among us, judging sin in his own people, saving by victory. The reference, cryptic to our ears nowadays but very plain to the Sanhedrin's ears, points up the two voices and accuses the Sanhedrin. 'You haven't sung the song of praise and honour; you've sung the song of complaint. Like the lone voice, out of tune with truth, you've sung the song of rejection.'

They'd already heard this reference when, in similar vein, Peter picked up this thread and wove it into his own denunciation of the Sanhedrin and their cronies. 'You disowned the Holy and Righteous One and asked that a murderer be released to you' (Acts 3:14). The Righteous One came among you and you, who want to be righteous ones, betrayed and murdered him.

Stephen blasts at them again with reference to the law – that great basis of their claim to moral superiority over all the nations. You have the law, you follow its rules to the grave, but in reality you disobey it. You break it with every breath that comes from within you.

It all adds up to the most damning set of charges that the Sanhedrin has ever heard. Every idol in the pantheon of pride has been demolished. Every bolt-hole down which the accused conscience might flee has been blocked. If they concede any of what Stephen has said, they are finished; their utter and total bankruptcy will be inescapable, they will be completely undone as a moral and spiritual power. It is the most humiliating exposure that they could suffer; every charge against God's people in the Old Testament is laid at their door.

What Does All This Have to do With Us?

Everything. First, we need to be careful that we don't dodge the sermon ourselves. We have to be prepared to stand under it as they did; in fact more so, for we should want the word of God to test us. We should have an automatic willingness to place ourselves under the scrutiny of the Scriptures, no matter who preaches them. Think for a moment of Psalm 139. Towards the close of the Psalm, David prays against wickedness in the land. He is faced by misuse of the name and the word of God (Ps. 139:20). Although his blood boiled with anger at what he saw around him, he also recognised the weakness of own soul, and that he too could harbour wickedness. So he prayed, 'Search me, O God, and know my heart; test me and know my anxious thoughts. See if there is any offensive way in me' (verses 23,24a). Like David, we can be led astray; like him, our only hope for protection against our ways becoming offensive to God is in God himself. So he goes on to pray 'and lead me in the way everlasting' (verse 24b). We can't sit back and say 'Go for it, Stephen, blast them!' careless of our own failings.

What Stephen says to the Sanhedrin searches our souls also. Do we not find precisely the same temptations now as the Sanhedrin faced then? Do we not have a new humanity that, though converted, shows tendencies similar to theirs? Like them, we can react badly when someone points out to us that we've created idols out of the things that God has given us, rejecting God himself.

We are just as capable of rejecting God's message as well as his messengers. The ways that we protect can be just as full of pride as theirs, or full of lust or envy or complacency. We can justify almost anything to ourselves if we want it badly enough. Or worse, unable to justify some of our conduct or attitudes, we still refuse to let anyone challenge them. So we excuse our waywardness, or we shut our ears to the voices that challenge us. That budding extra-marital affair ('Oh yes, I know where those conversations are heading, and quite like the idea'); a little creative accountancy at work ('Well, everyone does it'); dabbling with pornography ('It's harmless, and don't you dare tell me otherwise'). A Christian who has committed to a path that they know is wrong can become aggressively and uncharacteristically defensive, pro-testing too much that there's nothing wrong. That change of character betrays the secret choice and the guilty conscience. The inside shows.

Secondly, some of what we've seen so far in this book is reinforced here in this episode: Stephen, worked upon by the Holy Spirit, is doing the works that Jesus did. He certainly seizes the moment with both hands. He comes across religious resistance within the Sanhedrin's hearts. He also is, in a sense, catching up with God, since it is the work of God to break the Sanhedrin's grip upon the people and upon their access to God. God is certainly giving all that Stephen needs. The Spirit supplies all the wisdom and courage, the verses and quotes, the construction that inexorably drives home the point: everything that Stephen needs.

But new elements of God's work emerge. Being a fellow-builder with God means that we will be equipped and used by him correctly to handle the word of truth. I put it that way because the Sanhedrin had been, for all their lives, incorrectly handling the word of truth. They had done nothing but mishandle it. They had made it their own word, manipulating and twisting it. They had repeatedly put their own spin on it. They had mishandled the word of truth in order to build both righteousness and a truth regime for themselves. They held and shaped the very word of God in order to build something – albeit with some holy intentions – of their own design, that would ultimately be a testimony to them. Recall that Stephen had drawn the parallel with David, who decided he would build something for God. By stark contrast, God's fellow-builders let God build his house with his word. God's fellow-builders properly wield the sword of the Spirit in the power of the Spirit to the glory of God. It is not the sword of the church nor of the leadership; it is not the sword of the organisation nor the evangelist or pastor; it is nobody else's sword, save God's. It's his word, not ours. It is his power, not ours. Stephen's speech shows us this not simply by its content, but also by the way in which it is delivered: in the power of the Spirit. He correctly handled the word of truth.

He honoured God with courageously faithful witness. I was on another summer beach mission team, which benefited from a number of well-educated young men with a sophisticated sense of humour. There was also a young man on the team who was not going to get to university, however much he might have wanted to. Some of the team enjoyed plenty of laughs at his expense. But then this happened. Wednesday was 'Beach Barbecue' evening. It gave us a chance to preach the gospel. Mid-evening, a group of Hell's Angels rode down the hill and parked their bikes. They sat on a wall at the back of the beach and stayed through the 'epilogue' (the gospel talk at the end of the fun). Spiritual warfare looked more likely than spiritual conversation: they looked ready to rip off a few chicken's heads, which is what everyone knew Hell's Angels did for a lark of a Wednesday night. In our growing unease we reckoned that this was not the time for prolonged one-to-one evangelism, so after the epilogue had finished and we had handed out a respectable number of tracts, we all started drifting off. (Well, perhaps 'drifting' does not quite capture the sense of urgency and direction with which we moved.) As we headed for our supper, I looked back at the beach and saw the team member, who was the butt of jokes and who, as it happened, was called Stephen, walk straight up to the line of Hell's Angels. He stood in front of them and preached. He told them that they needed to repent. All our stupid cleverness fell away. He honoured God with courageously faithful witness. I don't know what happened to him in the years since then, but I'll never forget the sight of him doing that.

In front of Judaism's scare-squad, God's fellow-builder honoured God with courage; Stephen showed faithfulness to him and not to people; he honoured God with witness, not self-serving cleverness. As we will see, it cost him his life. The word 'witness' really does mean 'martyr'.

To ponder

- Is it an evangelistic embarrassment to you to have to speak of the God who judges?
- Do you struggle with the notion of God's wrath? If so, what is it in particular that bothers you and why?
- You might not have a confrontational personality, but are you capable of calling a spade a spade when it comes to sin and guilt before a holy God? What militates against us doing this? How does love for rebels translate into warning them about 'the wages of sin'?
- Could you describe ways in which our own culture has rejected God?

Chapter 6

God Builds by Death

The Martyrdom of Stephen

When they heard this, they were furious and gnashed their teeth at him. But Stephen, full of the Holy Spirit, looked up to heaven and saw the glory of God, and Jesus standing at the right hand of God. 'Look,' he said, 'I see heaven open and the Son of Man standing at the right hand of God.' At this they covered their ears and, yelling at the top of their voices, they all rushed at him, dragged him out of the city and began to stone him. Meanwhile, the witnesses laid their clothes at the feet of a young man named Saul. While they were stoning him, Stephen prayed, 'Lord Jesus, receive my spirit.' Then he fell on his knees and cried out, 'Lord, do not hold this sin against them.' When he had said this, he fell asleep. And Saul was there, giving approval to his death. On that day a great persecution broke out against the church at Jerusalem, and all except the apostles were scattered throughout Judea and Samaria. Godly men buried Stephen and mourned deeply for him. But Saul began to destroy the church. Going from house to house, he dragged off men and women and put them in prison (Acts 7:54–8:3).

Stephen has stood his ground in the face of his enemies, not as an individual but as a representative of all the Christians in Jerusalem. Behind the animosity that so hideously engulfs them lies a vast reservoir of hatred towards the name of Jesus. Yet instead of putting a spin on his faith in order to save his neck, Stephen has spoken with boldness about God's Son and about the Sanhedrin's attitude to him. In this, one member of the fellowship has stood for all. His conduct has said 'This is what followers of Jesus believe.' He has exalted Christ with his life; he is about to die for it, and Christ will be exalted again.

This is a profoundly serious moment for the church in Jerusalem. As we've noted, there has been persecution up until now, but so far no-one has actually died because of what they believe. But it is a defining moment for the life of the church all over the world and for all time.

We see for the first time here the kind of spirit that has been among us ever since. It is the spirit which C T Studd voiced. He was challenged as to why, against doctor's advice and despite his age, he was returning to what was then the Belgian Congo where he would almost certainly die in the proclamation of the gospel. He replied, 'If Jesus Christ be God and died for me, no sacrifice can be too great for me to make for him.' It is the spirit in which thousands upon thousands have given their lives rather than gain the approval of the world's powers. It is estimated that last century, more Christians were martyred than in all the preceding centuries put together. Cost what it may, glad faithfulness to Christ has been worth more to the people of God than anything that the world can offer. But it is not simply that martyrdom happens. It is that by it, God builds his house. To be a fellow-builder might mean that you build by death. As we see with Stephen.

Exalting Christ by Death

One question before we look at Stephen. Why is Christ exalted in the death of his people at the hands of his enemies? After all, it doesn't look like a win, does it?

There are several aspects to the exaltation of Christ in this way.

Christ is honoured by his people when, faced with the stark choice, they show that he means more to them than life itself. But it isn't simply that he is shown to be worth more than life; it is that he is so highly valued by those who were once his enemies. We claimed his throne for ourselves, declaring that we counted him worth nothing and ourselves worth everything. When his 'worth' is proclaimed by once-rebellious sinners dying out of loyalty to him, the power and glory of his redemptive love are declared. Once, Stephen neither knew of Christ nor cared for him. He did not worship him or serve him. Now he is ready to die for him. What but the power of God and the love of God could so profoundly and totally recreate a man that he will forfeit his own life for the name of Jesus?

There's more. In laying down his life for the glory of God, Stephen mirrored the Son who lays down his life for the glory of the Father. Of course, Stephen's death has absolutely no redemptive effectiveness whatsoever, but in that the Son's faithful *obedience* to the Father took him to death, so Stephen, and every martyr since, has reflected the love of the Son for the Father.

We might miss the beauty of this if we only ever think of Jesus dying for us. It is natural that we should only think of this; after all, our nature tends to be fairly self-centred. But we are not the only ones that he had in mind. He died on our behalf, that is, in our place; but he also died for the sake of the Father's name and honour, for the sake of the mission of God in the world. He was not killed upon the command of Satan; he laid down his life out of obedience to the will of the Father. This is what the Bible means when Christ is not only praised but also held before us as an example of humble obedience to the Father, even when it took him as far as death on a cross.

It is not merely obedience that bears the hallmarks of Christ; it is the obedient *faith* with which Stephen dies that bears Christ's stamp too. In Psalm 116, the psalmist described himself as God's servant. Though 'entangled by the cords of death', he trusts God. Though afflicted (verse 10) he does not turn away from God but believes. And though he thanks God for deliverance from his enemies, he acknowledges that even if God had not spared him, his death would not have meant that his life was worthless to God. Far from it: for 'Precious in the sight of the LORD is the death of his saints' (Ps. 116:15). In life, he has faith in God; and he will trust in the goodness of God even in death. One day, another servant would come. Like the unknown songwriter who gave us Psalm 116, he would not turn away from the God who allowed his servant to die. He too would trust the God who had said that his servants are precious to him; and so die believing. As Stephen faces death with obedient faith, the image of Christ is reflected. And every reflection of Christ exalts him.

There's even more to it than obedient faith. Such obedient faith comes from *love*; it is love that seeks to honour God. To count God's honour as of higher worth than your own life is to use the accountancy of love. The good of the one that you love is worth everything that you might have to give up, when you love that person more than yourself.

It is the martyrs' love that John sees in his apocalyptic vision of the victorious church that I mentioned earlier, in

Revelation 12. The dragon, Satan, is poised to devour the Christ at the moment of his birth but he is thwarted: the child is snatched up to the throne of heaven. The shocking birth-scene gives way to visions of battles, of warfare between the foiled, frustrated evil one and God. The first battle is in heaven; it sees him defeated again and hurled down to earth. Back down here he hounds the woman who gave birth to the child; again he loses. Enraged and furious he takes his warfare to the church, the other offspring of the woman. He loses again, but driven by unalloyed hate, he continues his attempts to wipe out the people of God. He will keep losing. In this vivid drama, two things are found on earth which defeat Satan when he battles against heaven. The first is the cross and the second is the love that God's people have for Jesus. 'They overcame him by the blood of the Lamb and by the word of their testimony; they did not love their lives so much as to shrink from death' (Rev. 12:11). If we can put it like this, there is something in loving God more than our own lives that means we will die rather than be disloyal to him, and that love strengthens heaven. We win because heaven loves us; and in the glorious mutuality of love between the Lord and his people, heaven wins because we love the One enthroned there.

There's one more aspect to this. Christ is exalted in our life-losing service because by facing death for him we acknowledge the truth, the reality of our situation. The reality that defies our desperate-not-to-die world is that we're already dead.

In the face of everything that the world calls life, the Christian says, 'This is not really life; this is a shadow of life. The real thing is life in Jesus, life that you only reach through death in Jesus.' One of those involved in Stephen's death, Saul of Tarsus, was later to write, 'Now if we died with Christ, we believe that we will also live with him' (Rom. 6:8). His testimony to the Christians in Galatia was, 'I have been crucified with Christ and I no longer live, but Christ lives in me. The life I live in the body, I live by faith in the Son of God, who loved me and gave himself for me' (Gal. 2:20). To the church in Colosse, he would write, 'you died, and your life is now hidden with Christ in God' (Col. 3:3). How can those who once belonged to a world that dodges death and even body-swerves the topic, willingly and calmly endure agonising death for the sake of the name and kingdom of Jesus Christ? Because, as Isaac Watts put it in an infrequently sung verse of *When I survey the wondrous cross*:

His lifeblood, like a crimson robe,
Clothes all his body on the tree:
Then I am dead to all the globe,
And all the globe is dead to me!

Thus the martyrs are honoured in Hebrews 11:

Others were tortured and refused to be released, so that they might gain a better resurrection. Some faced jeers and flogging, while still others were chained and put in prison. They were stoned; they were sawn in two; they were put to death by the sword. They went about in sheepskins and goatskins, destitute, persecuted and ill-treated – the world was not worthy of them (Heb. 11:35–38).

Thus saints have gone to the stake. Consider some of their words. This is from Ignatius, Bishop of Antioch:

Now I begin to be a disciple. I care for nothing, of visible or invisible things, so that I may but win Christ. Let fire and the cross, let the companies of wild beasts, let breaking of bones and tearing of limbs, let the grinding of the whole body, and all the malice of the devil, come upon me; be it so, only may I win Christ Jesus!

Consider this account of the martyrdom of the Bishop of Smyrna, Polycarp:

> After feasting the guards who apprehended him, he desired an hour in prayer, which being allowed, he prayed with such fervency, that his guards repented that they had been instrumental in taking him. He was, however, carried before the proconsul, condemned, and taken to be burnt in the market place. The proconsul then urged him, saying, 'Swear, and I will release thee; reproach Christ.' Polycarp answered, 'Eighty and six years have I served him, and he never once wronged me; how then shall I blaspheme my king, Who hath saved me?'

These are the final moments on earth of John Philpott, of whom almost no-one these days has heard: he was the son of a knight, born in Hampshire, and brought up at New College, Oxford. On 17 December 1555, he was told that he was to die next day. Arriving at the stake, he said, 'Shall I disdain to suffer at the stake, when my Redeemer did not refuse to suffer the most vile death upon the cross for me?'[2]

Their spirit echoes in our own day through the stories of countless Christians.

Thirty-four-year-old Jiang Zongxiu was arrested by police in China's south-western Guizhou province on 18 June 2004 on a charge of 'spreading rumours and inciting to disturb the social order'. What she had been doing was distributing Bibles in the street. During her interrogation she was beaten and kicked until she died. This was the first-hand report of her mother-in-law who had been arrested at the same time, but was later released. Friends and relatives attested to Mrs Jiang's good health before her arrest.

On 30 June 2004 a Taliban spokesman contacted the press agency Reuters to announce the death of Maulawi Assadullah, a former Muslim cleric who had been sharing his new Christian faith in the Awdand district of Ghazni Province, Afghanistan. According to the spokesman, Abdul Latif Hakimi, 'A group of Taliban dragged out Maulawi Assadullah and slit his throat with a knife because he was propagating Christianity. We have enough evidence and local accounts to prove that he was involved in the conversions of Muslims to Christianity.'[3]

We watch Stephen, and we discern the spirit of all witnesses. If we would be God's fellow-builders we have to come to terms with this kind of Christianity for ourselves, whether or not the church where we live faces such furious persecution. We don't come to Christ and pick which discipleship course we're going to go on: the martyr's course or the safe course. Nor are there different species of Christian. What Stephen shows is simply the spirit that Christ showed; Christ who, in Revelation 3:14, is called the 'faithful and true witness'.

Stephen's Death: The Confrontation Between Heaven and Hell

We notice first of all that here is a bare-fisted knuckle fight between heaven and hell. That conflict envisaged in Revelation 12 is this one and every other like it.

Notice the anger in the gnashing of teeth. Most of the other New Testament references to this have to do with anguish – the anguish and remorse of those who experience the judgement of God. Here, it follows the kind of use that we find in two of the Psalms. In Psalm 35:16 and 37:12 the fury of the unrighteous and the unjust is aimed at God's servant. The first of these could almost have been written for Stephen: 'They slandered me without ceasing. Like the ungodly they maliciously mocked; they gnashed their teeth at me. O Lord, how long will you look on? Rescue my life from their ravages, my precious life from these lions' (Ps. 35:15–17). The rage of the leaders takes on a horrifically violent form that expresses a satanic and de-humanising malevolence.

Further, notice in Acts 7:57–58 how they cover their ears. Why are they doing that? Because they do not want to hear what, through Stephen, God is saying. They are in such rebellion against God that they have become painfully sensitised to his word. It is offensive and excruciating for them to hear the voice of God's servant. 'The world' here is not comfortable with Stephen and physically tries to block out the sound of the preacher. Satan is called 'the father of lies' and 'the accuser of the brothers'. Having used lying witnesses, and having failed to counter Stephen's message, they cannot now bear the sound of the truth.

It gets worse: they start yelling at the top of their voices and running at Stephen. Remember, this is the Sanhedrin. This is the nobility, the leaders of the great and influential families in Judah. These are the chief priests and the scribes; these are dignitaries. Yet look at what they have become. They, who were so keen to avoid any kind of civil disturbance lest the Romans clamp down, have completely lost it. They introduce an element of chaos and civil unrest, the like of which has not been seen before. So they become like wild animals. Yelling at the tops of their voices, they all rush at him and, propelled by the one who was from the beginning a murderer, they murder Stephen.

So what comes from heaven for Stephen?

From heaven comes the Spirit to fill Stephen. Wonderful! We know that Stephen is full of the Spirit and of wisdom and faith. But now the Spirit comes to him again: 'Stephen, full of the Spirit'. That fullness of the Spirit is the most sustaining and fortifying of all the blessings from heaven. Being filled, there's no room left for anything else.

When the Lord sees that we need him, he gives himself again to fill us. Notice the terms carefully: 'full of the Spirit'. It's God himself who fills Stephen. It's not the gifts of the Spirit here, nor the graces: Stephen is filled right up with the Spirit himself. We need him when hell is let loose against us. We need more than gifts, more than graces: we need God himself, who is the only Victor over hell. So as evil breaks loose against Stephen, God comes to him in the Spirit. Faster than the wicked can cover the ground between the Sanhedrin and Stephen, God comes to his servant's aid. God is very good, very kind, very *quick*.

We read more: Stephen is not only filled with God the Spirit, but heaven catches his gaze. 'But Stephen, full of the Holy Spirit, looked up to heaven and saw the glory of God, and Jesus standing at the right hand of God' (7:55). He looks up and sees heaven opened. What does he see there – what does God give Stephen a sight of to be captivated by? He sees the dazzling brilliance of God's holiness and power; he sees Jesus standing at the right hand of God. Yet while Stephen sees his own destination, he is not really gripped by his own impending glory: he is shown the glory of God. It is so instructive. We need to see the glory of God to get us through trials. The prospect of our own glory is wonderful, but to see the glory of God is so much more important in the psyche of the Christian. Why? Because there is something in us that is satisfied and strengthened when we glimpse the glory of God. We are remade in Christ in such a way that we respond to God's glory more than we respond to anything or anyone else. He is our life. He is our hope. He is our glory. We might not think this of ourselves as we exhibit what can be depressingly frequent failings, but God has made us so that seeing him is enough to get us through anything.

Stephen sees not only the glory of God, he clearly sees Jesus standing there 'at the right hand of God the Father'. What is the significance of that? It shows him the One who is in control. The power rests in heaven, not with these defeated and deranged men. Notice that the vision of where the power lies, in the hands of his beloved Jesus, simply comes to him as a gift. He doesn't have time to ask for it. He hasn't had time to go away and read books or listen to sermons to get the teaching, as if by getting teaching he will see this. It's simply given to him in the instant. Faster than evil can engulf him, God is there. Before the malicious get near him, before these men have even picked up a stone, God is there. Richard Keen's hymn is apt:

> Fear not, He is with thee, O be not dismayed;
> For He is thy God, and will still give thee aid:
> He'll strengthen thee, help thee, and cause thee to stand,
> Upheld by His righteous, omnipotent hand.
>
> The soul that on Jesus has leaned for repose
> He will not, He cannot, desert to its foes;
> That soul, though all hell should endeavour to shake,
> He never will leave, He will never forsake.

Whatever the devil does to us in this life, though he does his worst, it is not enough to separate us from God. In fact (and here is the truly staggering thing) God, as he does here, turns the worst that Satan can do right around for our greatest blessing. Do you think Stephen had ever had an experience with God like that before? I don't think so. The very onrush of hell is itself the occasion for Stephen being shown all this glory.

And as the devil revealed his hand through the attitude of the Sanhedrin, heaven shows its hand in the attitude of Stephen. The likeness of Christ in his people is so clearly seen and heard as Stephen utters his final words. 'While they were stoning him, Stephen prayed, "Lord Jesus, receive my spirit." Then he fell on his knees and cried out, "Lord, do not hold this sin against them." When he had said this, he fell asleep' (7:59,60). Neither self-preoccupation nor bitterness are here, only the image and echo of Christ.

Stephen's death is all about Christ. It is for the sake of Christ's name and his cause, which is what the opposition has focused on. It is endured in the strength of Christ: Christ who strengthens him by the Spirit, Christ who stands in sovereignty, protecting Stephen not from physical death but from the terrors of evil. It displays the likeness of Christ by what's felt and prayed.

It's all about Christ. If your life is all about Christ, then martyrdom is just the next step in such a life, should God so order your circumstances. If your life is all about Christ, you've ceased to be number one. You've already died with him, and you've made a decision to lay down your life daily as you follow him – you have taken up your cross to follow him. Stephen had already died to himself and to the terror, or the approval, of men. In Christ, he was fully alive to God.

There's one more glorious aspect to this moment. In apparent defeat at the devil's hands, heaven wins again. This is the reality of martyrdom that carnal minds will never understand: that when the devil did his worst to

Stephen, all it did was to send Stephen to where God wanted him to be. Back to Psalm 35: David continues:

> I will give you thanks in the great assembly; among
> throngs of people I will praise you . . .
> Do not be far from me, O Lord.
> Awake, and rise to my defence!
> Contend for me, my God and Lord.
> Vindicate me in your righteousness, O LORD my God; do
> not let them gloat over me.
> Do not let them think, 'Aha, just what we wanted!' or say,
> 'We have swallowed him up.'
> May all who gloat over my distress be put to shame and
> confusion; may all who exalt themselves over me be
> clothed with shame and disgrace . . .
> My tongue will speak of your righteousness, and of your
> praises all day long' (Ps. 35:18-28).

God defended Stephen; he vindicated and rescued him not by saving his skin, but by taking him to the greatest assembly where an innumerable throng praises the Righteous One.

What a loser the devil is – he kills God's servant, and it all works out well for that servant! In fact, it couldn't have worked out better. There is a dynamic about the Christian life that means that the more the devil piles on, the more God turns it around for good. Not just for good, but for glory and blessing. Remember what Paul writes in 2 Corinthians 4:17? 'For our light and momentary troubles are achieving for us an eternal glory that far outweighs them all.' What's going on here? Is God working for us an eternal weight of glory *despite* the persecution? No! The affliction *itself* is working the glory. And notice the 'multiplier effect': short-lived troubles produce eternal glory; light troubles produce a far greater weight of glory. The devil piles on a kilo of affliction for a short while and the eternal glory goes up by a few thousand tonnes. Should we fear persecution? Not as much as we might. We shouldn't try and attract it, but we needn't cower away from it. We have natural fears of pain, embarrassment, social exclusion or ridicule but we needn't be paralysed by fear of the consequences.

Perhaps it is the case that we dread persecution more as we imagine it than when it actually comes our way. For in North Korea, Indonesia, Nigeria, and many other parts of the world, God seems to be doing now what he did then in Jerusalem: making his presence felt in such a way that courage outweighs danger and love outweighs death. And he does it in far less extreme situations. It's unlikely that you'll be shot in the office for being a Christian, but when you do bear brave testimony to God's truth, or to your own faith, he is present to multiply your courage, to give you peace and poise. Last night, after our Bible Study, one of our fellowship told me what happened to him a few days ago at work. Some of Ben's colleagues decided to have a go at him in the staff room. From out of the blue, hostility and accusations came flying at him. Derision poured out from those with whom, just ten minutes earlier, he'd been serving the public out on the shop-floor. Without losing his temper Ben replied, when he was given room for an edgeways word, and when he wasn't he shrugged his shoulders and carried on with his lunch. He stayed calm, yet he didn't back down and deny God. (This won't always happen, but later that afternoon the most argumentative of the colleagues apologised and then listened without a single objection as Ben described what God means to him.) Where was God? Right there in the shop, with his fellow-builder. What happened to the attack? God turned it right around to his glory and Ben's blessing.

The worst that the devil can do to you will be used by God to do precisely the things that the devil wants to prevent and that God is determined to accomplish: the building of his kingdom, the exaltation of his name and the blessing of his dearly loved fellow-builders. In the confrontation between heaven and hell, God always wins. He always has: look at the cross. In this lies the sure and certain hope of our salvation.

Death, Persecution and Eviction: Heaven Wins Again

'On that day a great persecution broke out against the church at Jerusalem, and all except the apostles were scattered throughout Judea and Samaria' (Acts 8:1).

Plants use 'dispersal strategies' for getting their seed or spores out there to spread the species. One of the strategies favoured by plants with pods, like peas or laburnum trees, relies on the pod drying out. It's really neat: the outside of the pod dries out more than the inside; the wind and the sun get to it more. As the pod dries differentially, it twists. The twisting force increases until it exceeds the strength of the walls of the dried-out cells that run along the outer join between the two halves of the pod. Suddenly the pod snaps open with sufficient force to fling out the seed. The boffins call it ballistic seed dispersal. Mushrooms do it too – have you ever noticed mushroom caps that seem to have been sprung inside out, like umbrellas in strong wind? As they suddenly invert, the spores held on those thin fin-like structures underneath are flung out onto the breeze. For the pod or the cap, it's very costly.

Stephen's costly death prompts the similarly ballistic dispersal of the church from Jerusalem. Believers are scattered, spore-like, into the world beyond the comfort of the fellowship in the heart-land. It looks disastrous, but look at the places that Luke tells us the spores landed: 'all except the apostles were scattered throughout Judea and Samaria'. Come across that before? Acts 1:8 'You will receive power when the Holy Spirit comes on you and you will be my witnesses in Jerusalem and in all Judea and Samaria and to the ends of all the earth.'

Of God's fellow-builders, Adam Clarke wrote:

> They work, and God works with them. The church is founded and built up. Its adversaries, with every advantage in their favour, cannot overthrow it. Is it impossible to look at this without seeing the mighty hand of God in the whole. He permits devils and wicked men to work to avail themselves of all their advantages yet he counterworks all their plots and designs, turns their weapons against themselves and promotes his cause by the very means that were used to destroy it.[4]

God uses this satanic blast on Stephen, and thereafter on all the church in Jerusalem, to scatter the seed and to fulfil what Jesus said. Stephen's death looks like a victory for hell, but it was heaven that won. The devil tries to wipe out the church in Jerusalem, and what happens? God uses it to fulfil the promise that he gave through Jesus Christ. The persecution results in a massive expulsion – there were thousands of believers in Jerusalem by now, it must have been an awesome sight; how did the authorities organise it? Such orchestrated evil, such efficient removals, such a thorough attempt to edit the church out of history. Yet Satan only ended up serving the purposes of God! There's an echo of the massively solid and unassailable sovereignty of God that we encounter in Psalm 2. The kings of the earth conspire and rage against the Lord and his anointed. But God laughs them to derision and warns them to pay him homage, rather than take him on: the scornful laughter can turn to destructive wrath. Everything that Satan tries to do against God, God flips right over and uses to his own ends. It must be murder being the devil.

But it is *costly* seed dispersal. It cost Stephen his life. It cost all the believers except the apostles their homes. Hastily gathered belongings, quick farewells, children crying; treasures must be left, routines and futures abandoned; circles of friends are broken, maybe family ties become unravelled. It cost them. Many were put to death, as Stephen had been, but even those who weren't killed had many smaller deaths to die in those catastrophic days.

It is rare to read a book on church planting that suggests that persecution, loss and death are the ways to do it. It would be an unusual plan for church growth that would read: 'Disrupt your children's education, lose your job, kiss goodbye to your pension; then have your neighbours turn against you and let the authorities evict you unlawfully. Get flung into prison. Have a few of the fellowship murdered. Then tell everyone how much God loves you.' But the story of the spread of the church in so many parts of the world involves some or all of these things. God's ways are not ours, neither are his thoughts ours.

But there's something else going on. The persecution that hits Jerusalem is worsened by a man who one day will become one of the church's most effective evangelists and inspired writers. A young man named Saul watched Stephen being stoned to death. People lay their clothes at his feet so that they can throw their stones more easily. Saul looks on, giving approval to Stephen's death. From then on, he tries 'to destroy the church. Going from house to house he drags off men and women and puts them in prison' (Acts 8:3). He becomes the chief opponent of the church, because he hates the great king and head of the church. Later, in an autobiographical passage in Acts, he would confess that: 'I too was convinced that I ought to do all that was possible to oppose' (notice what he says here – not to oppose the church but . . .) 'to oppose the name of Jesus of Nazareth. And that is just what I did in Jerusalem. On the authority of the chief priests I put many of the saints in prison, and when they were put to death, I cast my vote against them' (Acts 26:9,10).

It is in this volcanic persecution that God sets up Saul. This man, who will try to demolish the church and who persecutes Christ, will become the most astonishing example of the power and the grace of God as later he builds up the church and loves Christ. Do you see how God is setting the whole thing up for his greater glory? The devil loses again.

Don't miss this point. When we think of what it means to be a witness, we have to keep reminding ourselves to think strategically; to think not in terms of ourselves and our comfort, but to think in terms of what is going on with respect to the glory of God. It can be a struggle to keep remembering that God will turn everything that the devil does around, and use it for his own glory. But the devil will never win against God.

We need to see this in Stephen's martyrdom and its aftermath so that we do not lose sight of it in our own lives. If our horizons narrow right in to 'me and my comfort' we won't even begin to be witnesses in this world, let alone have a spirit of a witness that would take us to martyrdom. If we think that God's chief responsibility is to look after our material and physical comfort then we won't be witnesses. We'll just become self-preoccupied little Christians who sink into mediocrity and even bitterness. It is as we think *outside* ourselves, as we think of God's power and grace that we live differently.

As we see what God accomplishes through our suffering, we bear it with joy, as Paul wrote in Romans 5:3,4. As we think of the constant victory of God, we pray differently. Our instinctive prayer is that God would solve our problems for us. Instinctively we ask God to keep us safe all the time. I don't know if we've got any biblical warrant to pray that prayer at all; and anyway, he keeps on not doing it. He keeps on showing what seems to be a cavalier disregard for the comfort and physical, temporal well-being of his children. The problem is in our perspective. He has a complete regard for his glory and his glory is our true goal and our true and lasting safety. Whatever the devil tries, God will turn it round. The devil will always lose. But if we have set up the Christian life and 'victory' as inseparable from what the world would call comfort and success, then we'll hardly ever be witnesses like Stephen. We will want God's glory to be painted on too small a canvas.

May God grant us the desire to be his fellow-builders whatever the cost. May he give us that real life which is fired by a consuming passion to see his glory.

To ponder

- What little deaths might following Jesus cause for you?
- The 'already dead' idea – in what ways is it right for a Christian not to be part of this world, even though you're in it? Put it the other way round: can you be fully engaged in this world as a fellow-builder with God if you are no different from the world? What differences benefit the building process, and what differences might actually hinder it?

- Do you always have to come out on top? What might be gained by dying to yourself?
- How do you gauge progress and success in your Christian life and in the life of your church?
- Whatever hell does, heaven wins. Write down the disasters or difficulties that you face at the moment. Talk with a friend about how God could turn those around so that they work for his glory.
- I ask this question reverently, but what is God for in your life?
- What has recently flooded your life with the glory of Christ? Was it a comfortable experience? What did it cost you?

Chapter 7

Philip, Strangeness, and the Question of Who Really is the Messiah

God engaged Philip in cross-cultural mission. An increasing number of Christians are becoming engaged in the same kind of work here in Britain; the kind that, for instance, Friends International is so effective at both doing and encouraging. It involves communicating the gospel to 'internationals': folk who are over here, perhaps for a short time to study or on a short-term work contract. The intention is that by introducing them to the Lord Jesus Christ here, they can go back to their own country transformed and do the kind of 'gospel work' that others couldn't easily get into that country to do. It works on the principle that the best people to evangelise in, say, China, are in fact the Chinese.

Well, for Britain read Samaria and for Chinese read Ethiopian; and turn back the calendar by the best part of two thousand years.

We pick up the story at Acts 8:26.

Now an angel of the Lord said to Philip, 'Go south to the road – the desert road – that goes down from Jerusalem to Gaza.' So he started out, and on his way he met an

Ethiopian eunuch, an important official in charge of all the treasury of Candace, queen of the Ethiopians. This man had gone to Jerusalem to worship, and on his way home was sitting in his chariot reading the book of Isaiah the prophet. The Spirit told Philip, 'Go to that chariot and stay near it.' Then Philip ran up to the chariot and heard the man reading Isaiah the prophet.'Do you understand what you are reading?' Philip asked. 'How can I,' he said, 'unless someone explains it to me?' So he invited Philip to come up and sit with him. The eunuch was reading this passage of Scripture: 'He was led like a sheep to the slaughter, and as a lamb before the shearer is silent, so he did not open his mouth. In his humiliation he was deprived of justice. Who can speak of his descendants? For his life was taken from the earth.' The eunuch asked Philip, 'Tell me, please, who is the prophet talking about, himself or someone else?' Then Philip began with that very passage of Scripture and told him the good news about Jesus. As they travelled along the road, they came to some water and the eunuch said, 'Look, here is water. Why shouldn't I be baptised?' And he gave orders to stop the chariot. Then both Philip and the eunuch went down into the water and Philip baptised him. When they came up out of the water, the Spirit of the Lord suddenly took Philip away, and the eunuch did not see him again, but went on his way rejoicing. Philip, however, appeared at Azotus and travelled about, preaching the gospel in all the towns until he reached Caesarea (Acts 8:26–40).

The Story So Far: Persecution, Preaching and Growth

The gospel is spreading geographically. As we have noted already, it is spreading by the scattering of the church through the persecution that breaks out after the stoning of Stephen. So Acts 8:1–3. 'On that day a great persecution broke out against the church at Jerusalem, and all except the apostles were scattered throughout Judea and Samaria. Godly men buried Stephen and mourned deeply for him. But Saul began to destroy the church. Going from house to house, he dragged off men and women and put them in prison.'

But it is also spreading because those who were persecuted preached. They don't simply go to new places, ignore new people and say nothing about Christ in new situations. They don't lick their wounds, feel sorry for themselves and withdraw. Neither do they become reticent out of bitterness towards Christ for messing up their lives. Nor are they silenced by fear of what people might do to them. We say, 'Once bitten, twice shy.' These people were the opposite: bitten by the wild beast of affliction, they stick their heads back right in the beast's mouth: 'Go on, have another go if you will, I'm still going to speak!' They did not pull back having suffered persecution, but were spurred on all the more. Luke has already recorded Peter's reaction when forbidden to speak in the name of Jesus: it is a pattern for witnesses everywhere: 'We cannot help speaking about what we have seen and heard' (Acts 4:20).

The persecution in Jerusalem invigorates rather than dampens down the witness-bearing. The believers are not put off preaching: they are motivated for it! When they got somewhere, anywhere, they preached. Some of them might have settled; others, from that point on, might have led a wandering life, becoming itinerant evangelists. But wherever they went, they voiced the faith by preaching the word. Luke doesn't describe a kind of preaching that focused on persecution, and they don't appear to spend their time carping about the Sanhedrin:

they declare the gospel message. So 8:4, 'Those who had been scattered preached the word wherever they went.'

Relocated by God, they became fellow-builders with him as he enlarges his kingdom. But what was going on in these people that made them so astonishingly useful? What might we expect this same God, who is still on the same mission, to do in us? Luke dwells on the experiences of one man in particular. Of all those who were scattered, Philip's work receives the most attention. It has particular significance in the global growth of the church outward from its centre in Jerusalem. But it also has vital significance for us. What we learn from the story is that God writes his own rule book. Our place is not to tell him how to do it, but to be responsive to his direction; even when it's strange. And God does 'strange' like no-one else! We take up Philip's story at Acts 8:5.

Enter Philip

'Philip went down to a city in Samaria and proclaimed the Christ there. When the crowds heard Philip and saw the miraculous signs he did, they all paid close attention to what he said. With shrieks, evil spirits came out of many, and many paralytics and cripples were healed. So there was great joy in that city' (Acts 8:5–8).

One of those elements of the pattern of God's work that has been prominent in Acts so far has been that kingdom-builders seize the moment. When people came up to Peter after the man had been healed at the Gate Beautiful, he seized the moment and preached. In front of the Sanhedrin Stephen did the same. Here Philip, though a displaced victim, seizes the moment and preaches the word.

But, as we might guess, there's something else going on here. As the gospel spreads further out from Jerusalem the preaching is being done by believers other than the apostles. The apostles weren't made redundant, but the preaching was not ˙exclusively theirs. Back in Acts chapter 6, the apostles had simplified their workload down to preaching and prayer and had brought others in to get on with the other things that needed to be done. The ministers, if you like, concentrated on the ministry of the word and on prayer. But then the persecution starts. Those who are getting on with the other tasks are scattered, and the apostles are left back in Jerusalem.

What does God expect the scattered believers to do? Are they supposed to say, 'We can't preach, it's the apostles who do the preaching. We haven't been authorised by anybody; we haven't jumped through the hoops'? Not at all; God seems to have expected those whom he had intended to be scattered to get on with preaching. That dynamic is absolutely crucial in the building of God's house. God doesn't send Philip to Samaria so that Philip can sit there surrounded by opportunity, waiting for an apostle to come from Jerusalem to Samaria to start preaching. The apostles do come, but to a place where the work is already in progress.

That has two implications for us these days. First of all, we need to be careful about restricting work to a certified few. There are, of course, equal though opposite dangers in never checking what's happening, and of giving tasks to loose cannons. Yet these dangers do not sanction the 'professionalising' of something which is listed in Scripture as being among the Spirit's gifts. It is not to be seized upon by the church and constricted to a few in a particular location who have qualified according to the rest of the church's rubrics. When we avoid the dangers of chaos by creating an elite that is cordoned off by organisational structures and regulations, the church loses its capacity to do mission in a way that is responsive to both the situations that God puts us in and to the God who is the real missionary. Professional clericalism, which many of our denominations have enshrined, mine included, has been detrimental to the growth of the gospel in Scotland and in many other parts of the world. Discern those in whom God has placed a preaching gift, but don't tell God that it can only be effective when it is used by those to whom we have granted a particular job title.

The second thing, which perhaps has more relevance to most of us, is that if God has given *you* a hammer and he places *you* in front of a rock that needs to be broken, it might just be that, in the mysteries of divine providence, he wants *you* there to use the hammer. Gentler imagery might suit some situations more, but you get the point. He has not put you there to phone somebody else to come some distance and take the hammer that he's given *you*, and break that rock. He has made you who you are, has put you where you are, and has given you a gospel to communicate there. If God had wanted the vicar to be the only one to stand at the school gate with Samantha for over an hour after the kids have gone in, and speak to her about how much God cares for her and has done for her, God would have put the vicar there. And that would never have done because the vicar's a bloke who, though a nice chap, doesn't really understand how Samantha feels; and anyway, Samantha wouldn't open up to the vicar about her breast cancer the way she does to you. Samantha isn't really looking for someone with a theology degree. She doesn't want you to be fantastically eloquent; you don't have to be able to string together a wonderful mini-sermon that would impress the rest of the fellowship. But you do need to be willing to seize the moment that God has created for you and for his kingdom. Samantha speaks to you because she feels that you will care, listen and help.

If those who were scattered, as they are called in verse 4 of chapter 8, had reacted differently, all the persecution in the world wouldn't have brought the growth of the church.

Philip Who?

Just who is this man that God deploys on his expanding building site?

The spiritual and practical man

We start to get a picture of Philip as we pick up again on the delegation passage in Acts 6.

> Brothers, choose seven men from among you who are known to be full of the Spirit and wisdom. We will turn this responsibility over to them . . . This proposal pleased the whole group. They chose Stephen, a man full of faith and of the Holy Spirit; also Philip, Procorus, Nicanor, Timon, Parmenas, and Nicolas from Antioch, a convert to Judaism [who had then, we must conclude, been converted to Christianity]. They presented these men to the apostles, who prayed and laid their hands on them. So the word of God spread. The number of disciples in Jerusalem increased rapidly, and a large number of priests became obedient to the faith' (Acts 6:3–7).

Like Stephen, Philip is full of the Spirit. Being a spiritually minded and Spirit-enabled man, he is therefore full of wisdom. That is, he is a practically minded man, since wisdom is not primarily a matter of having deep thoughts; it's a matter of knowing what to do in a situation. In turn, therefore, he can be depended on. Somebody who claims to be full of the Spirit and is irresponsible isn't full of the Spirit. Somebody who is able to take on tasks and do them to the good of the church and the glory of God, such a person is genuinely spiritual. They won't just do a task, they will infuse the doing of it with the Spirit's graces. So in the situation described in Acts 6 they will make sure that the food gets to the people, but they won't just go around handing out food efficiently. Being full of the Spirit, they will literally minister; it will be an act of God's grace through them. So instead of slopping the widows' soup, or whatever, on the tables quickly so they've got that table done, they will serve at the tables with all the fruit of the Spirit: with the love, joy, peace, patience, kindness, goodness, faithfulness, gentleness and self-control that we read of in Galatians 5:22 and 23. Philip's practical work was suffused with the grace of God. What a man! What an absolute gem of a brother to have in the fellowship. Five such people in a church can utterly transform it. They are just so good to have around. They bring a breath of heaven.

The preaching man

But the spiritual and practical man becomes a preaching man, for God's fellow-builders are adaptable. We can use being 'practical' as an excuse for not speaking. It's as if we're taking the safe and easy route: to speak would be too challenging, so we'll just stick to what we know. Practical men can also be fearful men. Philip could have told himself 'I'm a practical man, therefore I can't speak.' But the 'therefore' would not have come from God. Philip, the practical and spiritual man becomes a preaching man. Such adaptability comes from being full of the Spirit who enables us for new situations. But it also comes from a concern, planted in our hearts by the Spirit, that the gospel should spread, that the lost should be saved, that Jesus should be honoured in the witness-bearing of his people.

Clearly, Philip had a gift for evangelism that was recognised later in his life by the church: by the time that Paul is making his way back to Jerusalem at the close of his third missionary journey, Philip is known as 'the evangelist' (Acts 21:8). God might not require all of us to preach, in the normal sense of that word, and he will not give the gift of being an evangelist to all of us, but we are all called to be witnesses. We are all called to communicate the truth not simply by lifestyle, relationship and character, but also with words. We don't get to ring-fence such a major area of life as speaking so that it can't be engaged in the growth of God's kingdom. Non-Christians around us are not psychic: they will not automatically grasp the content of the gospel just because we are nice people who happen to go to church. There is truth to be spoken. Philip is willing to obey whatever adaptations might be required. In fact, is it not the case that our gifts emerge *as* we obey the leading of the Spirit? Our gifts do not become apparent *prior* to such step-by-step responsiveness, as some kind of job title that we then start to 'fill'. Don't wait to have your gift-list written in the clouds. Get on with whatever comes to hand and then with the help of the fellowship, discern what gifts you have been shown to have.

The Kingdom comes to Samaria!

As the gospel spread into Samaria because of Philip's ministry it was flooding into a valley that had already been formed. A river had already flowed through

Samaria because a forerunner had already gone there with the gospel and with converting power. That forerunner was Jesus. The incident with the 'woman at the well' in John 4 has significance for the whole mission of God, as well as for her personally and for those in the town of Sychar. Jesus is taking the gospel outside the sphere of 'pukka' Judaism, into Samaria, the land of the compromisers.

A bit of background will help here. The relationship between Jews and Samaritans was as poor in the first century as it had ever been. The original rift happened a thousand years before, early in the reign of young, rash Rehoboam. As the kingdom split in two, the tribes of Judah and Benjamin stayed in the south, centred on Jerusalem; the remaining tribes went north under Jeroboam, and were centred in the city of Samaria. Since then, there had been deep-seated animosity between the two parts of the people of Israel. Samaria fell to the tyrannical Assyrian emperor Sargon in 722 BC, whose policy was to dissolve the energies of the vanquished by deporting them and mixing them with other peoples. The Samaritans never recovered either their racial or spiritual integrity and were from then on regarded by the southern kingdoms as being hopelessly compromised by polytheistic idolatry.

In later centuries they would antagonise the Jews further, opposing the rebuilding of Jerusalem by Nehemiah, building their own rival temple on mount Gerizim and joining the Seleucids in their war on the Jews. The Jews, for their part, regarded the Samaritans as totally disinherited from the nation that was 'the people' of God. Lumped together with the Philistines and the Idumeans, they were detested people, 'no nation'. No self-respecting Jew would have anything to do with them. This is, of course, the sharp point to the story of the

Good Samaritan. 'A *good* Samaritan? Mmmm, pigs might fly.' But John tells us that Jesus 'had to' go to Samaria with the gospel. In the telling of it at the well, he said to the woman there:

> 'Believe me, woman, a time is coming when you will worship the Father neither on this mountain nor in Jerusalem. You Samaritans worship what you do not know; we worship what we do know, for salvation is from the Jews. Yet a time is coming and has now come when the true worshippers will worship the Father in spirit and truth' (Jn. 4:21–23).

Jesus 'had to' go through Samaria. The necessity was not geographical – it wasn't as if there weren't any other roads – it was a compulsion that came from the mission of God, the command of the Father to take the gospel to the whole world. The 'had to' is because Jesus had to go and break down a barrier ahead of his disciples. He had to go through Samaria because the gospel had to reach the Samaritans. The king had come, and had to take his kingship to Samaria.

So what happens here is of massive significance. It is not that people from Samaria are converted so that they can go and worship in Jerusalem where the professionals are. The kingdom has come right there in Samaria as the gospel is preached, and as the people believe and turn to Christ. God is being worshipped in Samaria because the king is king anywhere.

Philip: The Man Who is 'Leadable'

Evangelism and church growth are going great guns in Samaria. Peter and John come from Jerusalem. They lay hands on people and the Spirit is given in a kind of

Samaritan Pentecost that parallels the one in Jerusalem. Wonderful!

Then God does strange stuff. In fact, he does wrong stuff; he does what all the church growth models say that you must not do. God takes Philip right out of Samaria and sends him somewhere else. 'No, No, Lord! He's supposed to stay there! He's got to set up a few churches, build a few buildings, obviously – you can't have a proper church without a building. At the very least, Lord, especially since he's the responsible type, he's got to run a few follow-up courses. He's got to produce materials for their discussion groups.' But no, Philip doesn't have to do that. It's not that such things are always and in every place to be bypassed by those who are Spirit-led. It's simply that God requires Philip to be responsive to him. God has something else for Philip to do, and *God* is not to be programmed by our models of good practice. Let God be God, or for all the responsible leadership in the world, you'll end up *mis*leading the people of God.

How do you think Philip would react? Do you think he would say, 'I can't go because there's work to do here'? This is a wise man. You'd think that a wise, practical man, having done the church planting, would stick around long enough to oversee the church building. But he is doing what Proverbs tells us to do: not to lean on our own understanding. So the wise man is wise enough to follow God even when it might not seem, from the earthly point of view, to be the obvious thing to do. The core of wisdom is to discern God's thing to do in a situation and then do it. Wisdom does not begin with the ability to generate plans but with the fear of the Lord.

God says, 'I want you to go south to the desert road that goes down from Jerusalem to Gaza.' God wants him to go somewhere where there isn't anybody. He doesn't tell him that an Ethiopian eunuch is on his way. He just tells him to go to the road to the desert. What's he going to find there? It's like telling someone to go up some track in the middle of the highlands of Scotland or the outback of Australia, when they are in the middle of a revival in Aberdeen or Adelaide. But that's what God does.

Then we have these marvellous four words at the beginning of Acts 8:27; 'So he started out.' Philip didn't wait for all the details. He didn't wait for the reasons before he started out. He didn't wait until he understood everything. 'On his way' he met the Ethiopian eunuch. He was prepared to start and see what God would do, on the assumption – an assumption that is part and parcel of reverence – that God is wise and that God has perfect plans. It was only when he was on the way that he discovered what it was all about.

There are times when we have asked God, 'What on earth am I *here* for? Why on earth have you placed me with these people at work? What on earth have you given me these neighbours for? Why have you put me in this church?' And then, suddenly, things have clicked into place. Suddenly you meet somebody, you have a conversation, something happens and you know why you're there. Dennis Lennon, who was the minister at St Thomas' Corstorphine and then became the adviser in evangelism for the diocese of Sheffield, had been a missionary with the Overseas Missionary Fellowship in South Thailand. While there, he had completely open access to the Kalantan-speaking North Malayans. They couldn't be reached with the gospel in their native territory, but over the border in Thailand there was no barrier, save learning the Kalantan dialect, which Dennis did.

Later, having left South Thailand, he was serving in St Barnabas Church in Cambridge and wondering why on earth he was there. Why on earth had God taken him from this fruitful work among the Kalantan, with huge potential, and put him in Cambridge? It's an extremely natural and perplexing question to have banging around unanswered in your mind, and it can weigh so heavily on the heart. But then one sunny morning, as he was simply standing on the street near the church, there came down the road, dressed in brightly colourful Kalantan dress, a group of Kalantan students who were in Cambridge for language training. On a street in Cambridge these young folk bumped into one of the few men in the whole of England who could speak to them in their own native dialect. From that God-created moment sprang a remarkable work among international students, and in that moment Dennis knew why he was there.

'So Philip started out and on his way . . . ' Why do you have this group of friends, or that particular set of colleagues? You may not know now; but go on being the witness that they need; go on obeying the Lord; go on responding to those nudges that he gives you. Don't wait for the outcome to be written in smoke in the sky. Don't wait for someone else to come up to you to say this is why you are here. Follow those hunches: speak to that person, listen to the other person, and share the gospel with another person as the Spirit prompts you. And having started out on the way, you will discover why you're on that particular road.

Some people take the 'let's panic' approach to hill-walking. If they can't actually see the path running ahead as far as the horizon, they'll assume that they're lost and stop in paralysed panic. It's really an approach to hill-*standing*. But often you have to walk on round a corner or over a rise in order to see the path. Some of us feel the need to see the end of a course of action before we will start at the beginning. In parts of life this is good – but not in all of life with God. It can be a measure of our personal

insecurity as much as of our wisdom. It can be a measure
of our pride in 'working everything out'. It can be a
simple matter of not having a risk-taking temperament.
But if we make obedience conditional upon our
recognition of the significance of a course of action, we
are usurping God's place in our lives. By one means or
another we become the Lord of the work. We become a
Messiah to the work of God, as if our place was the
supremely significant one.

Is God calling you to move, speak, and take new steps
for him? You have to start out. Don't assume that you
must see the significance of what you're being called to
before you go and do it. Like Philip, we discover the
significance of what God calls us to by obedience to the
call. Don't wait to know everything before you set off.

The Ethiopian: A Man Who is Seeking

Philip goes into the desert, and along comes a chariot.
Out of the blue, the Spirit gives Philip a command.
Whether it comes by an audible voice or a physical nudge
or an inner conviction so strong it doesn't need words,
we don't know; but we do know that it is clear. We also
know that it is bizarre. When I stand by the side of the
road and see a car go by, I rarely, indeed never, feel the
urge to go and run alongside it and bear witness to
Christ. In fact, I dissuade people – principally my
children – from running in traffic. Evangelistic jay-
walking has little to commend it. Pray for the people in
the cars and buses if you must, but stay on the pavement.
Yet Philip, who has not yet read the remaining verses of
Acts 8, and so doesn't know how it's all going to work
out, and who certainly wouldn't have known who is in
the chariot, is told by the Spirit of God to 'Go to that

chariot and stay near it.' He's not told to get in (armed robber – bad witness!) and the word 'stay' rather than 'stand' means that the chariot keeps moving so that Philip has to run with the chariot. So leadable Philip obeys. This responsible, grown adult actually does it! And *then* the significance, the staggering implication of all this prompting and obedience, becomes clear. The passenger is reading out loud. Sometimes it's easier to do that when you're reading a foreign language: he'd most likely be reading it in Hebrew. He is reading Isaiah the Prophet.

He is seeking spiritual answers. Was he discontented with the gods of Ethiopia and the religion that centred round the court of the Ethiopian queen Candace? He has obviously heard of the God of the Jews, and wanting to know more, he has gone up to Jerusalem to worship there at Passover, as many 'God-fearers' would have done. These were not Gentiles who had converted to Christianity; they simply wanted to come close to Judaism and Jehovah. He is going home with more questions than answers. So this high-ranking official, effectively the chancellor of Ethiopia, is reading.

He is seeking answers because the living God is seeking him. The hound of heaven is pounding along that road from Jerusalem to Gaza and is after this man. God sends an angel to the town in Samaria where he has been using Philip and tells him to leave: 'Go south to the road . . .' Then the Spirit tells Philip to go to the chariot and stay near it. God is after this man. God is on his mission to reach all nations. God is fulfilling what was spoken through Jesus back in Acts 1:8: 'But you will receive power when the Holy Spirit comes on you; and you will be my witnesses in Jerusalem, and in all Judea and Samaria, and to the ends of the earth.' God is after the best person to take the gospel to the nation of

Ethiopia – an Ethiopian. And he comes after him with a Bible and a Christian. What is he reading? Well, God has so worked it that the Ethiopian has brought the scroll of Isaiah. He is reading 'the fifth evangelist', the 'gospel of Isaiah'. In case we're in any doubt that the Spirit is at work, the eunuch just happens to be reading the John 3:16 of the Old Testament; Isaiah 53.

Philip opens with a question (always a good idea) and asks the best question that you could possibly think of in that situation, 'Do you understand what you're reading?' And the Ethiopian replies, 'How can I unless someone explains it to me?' What a cry, what a plea from a lost world to the world that has been found. What an invitation! So Philip gets in and explains just who and what the fourth 'Servant Song' in Isaiah is all about.

Look at what Philip does. A Bible is being read but not understood, so Philip explains it. Look at how he explains the passage. He doesn't get bogged down in arguments about how many Isaiahs there might have been. He doesn't launch into technicalities to do with the Hebrew. He doesn't launch into some sort of debate about the Jewish religion over and against the various Ethiopian religions. The question is, 'Who is this talking about?' So Philip tells him. He explains the gospel of Jesus Christ. 'Then Philip began with that very passage of Scripture and told him the good news about Jesus.' That little one-to-one Bible study could have gone anywhere but Philip kept it right on track. It was so beautifully simple. He just told the Ethiopian the good news about Jesus. And God caught him. The man became a Christian right there.

The Spirit has worked in a man who is leadable; he has brought into the drama a man who is seeking, with a Bible that gets explained so that Jesus is proclaimed. By verse 36 we have a man who wants to be identified with Christ in his death and his resurrection by means of baptism.

Who was responsible for the conversion of the Ethiopian eunuch? Just about everybody, in the providence and economy of God. We see Philip and the Ethiopian eunuch together in the chariot, but behind them lay all the un-named links in God's chain that made their meeting possible. We never know what God can use and the significance of it. We can never say that this moment, that day, this conversation, that act of kindness, or some part of just doing our ordinary daily work faithfully has been a useless waste, just because it didn't appear productive to us right there and then. God uses a long chain of people and events to bring these two together in the middle of nowhere. What you've done today might not be the end-point of such a chain; but that doesn't mean that you weren't link fourteen out of three hundred and seven. You might never know, but then you are called to walk by faith, to obey, to love, to do *all* things for Christ. Let him create the significance and even let others see it; your task, and your joy, is simply to serve the Lord in everything. Others might reap where you have sown; so be it if God is glorified.

God Does Even More Strange Stuff

Have you noticed how unpredictable God is?

> When they came up out of the water, the Spirit of the Lord suddenly took Philip away, and the eunuch did not see him again, but went on his way rejoicing. Philip, however, appeared at Azotus and travelled about, preaching the gospel in all the towns until he reached Caesarea (Acts 8:39–40).

God does another surprising thing: at the point of the Ethiopian's greatest pastoral need he whisks Philip away. We don't know for sure if Luke had ever watched an episode of *Star Trek*, but the word that he uses when he writes, 'suddenly took Philip away' is the Greek for 'to beam up'. For those among us given to these things, the verb is *harpadzo* and it means to snatch away. Interestingly, it's used in the Greek version of the Old Testament in Job 24:19 for the way that drought and heat evaporate the water that comes from melting snow. Philip probably wasn't vapourised, but 'suddenly', with no warning and very quickly, the Spirit of the Lord took Philip away and the eunuch could no longer even see him.

This is not the way to do it either. But it's the way that God did it.

Now the fact that God has taken Philip away, both in Samaria and here again with Philip and the Ethiopian eunuch, tells us something. Obviously it means that Philip's own evangelistic calling was to an itinerant ministry. But there is more to it than that, and the 'more' applies to all of us. It tells us that Philip was confident that God could look after those whom he had saved. Philip didn't behave as if he was the Messiah to these people and so had to stay with them. He was absolutely confident that God would be with them, and that the God who had given them life would sustain that life. He wasn't being irresponsible. He was doing what God told him to do, which is the ultimately responsible thing to do. He trusted God with these people, he did not entrust them to himself. This doesn't give us *carte blanche* to ignore people, and there are obvious defects in 'hit and run' evangelism that maybe we've all come across in one place or another. The issue is not whether this is the way it always *has* to happen everywhere, that as soon as somebody becomes a Christian you run as far away from them as possible. The issue is one of trust. Philip trusted God to look after those whom God had brought to new life through Philip. He did not, in the kingdom-building process, develop an overestimate of himself, as if the whole of their eternal destiny now depended on him. He was a midwife. He didn't try and become a mother to every baby that he brought into the world. And that meant that he had to trust God.

It also forces us to come to terms with the stark fact that God is unpredictable, and that he recreates an element of that in us when we follow the promptings of his Spirit. Jesus said it would be like that: 'The wind blows wherever it pleases. You hear its sound, but you cannot tell where it comes from or where it is going. So it is with everyone born of the Spirit' (Jn. 3:8). If you are a control freak, this sounds like nothing but trouble. But it is part of the control freak's struggle to yield to and ultimately rejoice in precisely this; the freedom of God.

Then, while Philip suddenly appears in the streets of Azotus (imagine the evangelistic impact of suddenly appearing out of thin air!), the Ethiopian 'did not see him again but went on his way rejoicing' (Acts 8:39).

He carries on back to the court of Queen Candace, where he has access to all Ethiopia since people will come to him from every corner of the nation. Talk about strategic evangelism! But whose was the strategy? It wasn't Philip's. It was God's. What did God have to do in Philip's life to involve Philip as a fellow-builder for his kingdom? He had to move Philip around; he had to make Philip leadable in ready obedience to the Spirit's inconvenient and unconventional guidance. God had to have a fellow-builder who wouldn't keep telling him what he could or couldn't do, who didn't think he knew better than God, and who didn't need to have all the answers. God used a servant who didn't think that he was the Messiah, so that the Servant who is the Messiah could work. Do we think that over the past two thousand years things have changed one tiny bit?

A Bigger Pattern For Our Humanity in Christ

The pattern of God's work in his fellow-builders grows and becomes richer. It is the developing picture of our humanity in Christ, of a humanity that is shaped by him just as his was shaped by the Father's will.

For God's fellow-builders, it is essential that we remember that God is building the house and not we ourselves. He brings us in on his building, but he doesn't absent himself and leave it to us. Neither does he build according to the dictates of his fellow-builders. He is the Builder. And he will write his own rule-book. Of course the builders have wisdom, they learn building; they are engaged in a process which, with God in the picture, makes sense. But it is God who writes his own rule-book: the builders do not tell God how it should be done. And yet it is one of our recurring problems that once God has used us to lay three or four rows of bricks we think we know all there is to know about brick-laying. We fancy ourselves as architects and engineers as well as master-builders. By the time we've put a few courses of bricks down, we think we know the whole building business and we go into consultancy mode with Jehovah as the client! We see one way of doing evangelism and we become set in it. We establish one pattern for church life or for an order of service on a Sunday morning, and we think we have nothing else to learn. We slip into one pattern of relating to the people around us at work and that's it: fixed until we or they leave. When we work in the 'God did it this way once so he'll always do it this way' mode, any true building stops. God writes his own rule-book. He tells his fellow-builders what to do, even if it seems insignificant and strange.

God uses leadable builders. The task of the fellow-builder is to be led in the building by the Master-builder. That requires a leadable heart, quick to respond to the voice of the Master-builder and yielded to the superiority of the Master-builder. A heart that really wants the building to go up whatever that's going to take.

Which leaves us where in our fellowships? With these questions: are we telling God how he's got to do his work or are we leadable? Is it God's work, or have we taken over? Is Jesus the Messiah, or have we adopted that role? Are we quick to sense and obey the voice of God? Are we open to the superiority of the Master-builder who is among us? Will we do what he asks even if it's not the way we would do it? Will we be like Philip, not in the sense that we do exactly the things that Philip did, but in the sense that we are as open as him to the strangeness and delight of the unpredictable God?

To ponder

- What puts you off trying something again that has been painful the first time? Should that be the determining thing? Why does it become so? What can stop it being so?
- At what times in your service of God have you felt that you didn't know what was going on in kingdom terms? Do you need to grade the significance of every possibility before you take it up? If so, what does that say to you about the way that you view the One whom you serve?
- Why has God put you where you are now? Think specifically of the people that you are with, the kind of

activities that you are engaged in, the gifts that God has given you and the needs of those around you. Anything to do with his mission? What, in particular?

- Can you live with disarray? Or are you a bit of a control freak? What impact will that have on the kind of ministry that you exercise? God seems to use both tendencies, but we can allow them to set the limits of what we think he might or might not do with our lives.

- Is there any place in your kingdom-building for following those nudges that the Spirit gives? Or are you more 'logical' and do you view them as part of a downward spiral into lunacy? Again, God uses people who have strongly intuitive ways of thinking, and those who like rational explanations of why they should do this and not that. What are the implications of your way of thinking for the kind of ministry that you exercise? And how do you work with fellow-builders who tend to think in the way that you don't? Do you respect them?

- In what ways can we become the Messiah to our kingdom-building, as if it all depended on us? What happens to us and to God's building work when that occurs?

- If you're the sort of person who likes to tie up every loose end in life, or finish everything to perfection, can you walk away from unfinished work in the way that Philip had to do? Do you always have a choice? And if not, how well do you cope when you have to do it?

The question returns: what, out of all the things that God did in these three fellow-builders, might he be doing in you at the moment? What will he have to do in days to come? What training is he giving you? What new attitudes does he want you to have? What old ones must you lose? Where is he taking you? To whom does he want you to speak?

****

He is on a mission and his mission is yours – no other mission can match his for its scope and vision, its delight and success, or its cost. And anyway, what other mission is there for the Christian to be on?

There is more to learn from the rest of Acts, in particular from the story of what God did with his profoundly gifted and terrifyingly bitter opponent Saul, who came from Tarsus. Coming soon, I hope, from a laptop near me to a bookshop near you.

Notes

1 Adam Clarke, *The Holy Bible, containing the Old and New Testaments* (New York, Carlton, 1857)

2 These accounts can be found in *Foxe's Book of Martyrs*

3 These two accounts are from *Barnabas*, the magazine of Barnabas Fund. September–October 2004. Visit www.barnabasfund.org. for more information. You might also want to visit www.csw.org.uk – the website of Christian Solidarity Worldwide, whose magazine *Release* gives up-to-date accounts of those persecuted for their Christian beliefs. *Witness* is the magazine of Release International, the UK arm of Voice of the Martyrs, founded by Pastor Richard Wurmbrand. Visit the website at www.releaseinternational.org. *Jesus Freaks* is a profoundly moving book of testimonies from the persecuted church. I recommend it strongly. dc talk and The Voice of the Martyrs, *Jesus Freaks: Stories of those who stood for Jesus* (Eagle Publishing, Guildford, 2003)

4 Adam Clarke, *The Holy Bible, containing the Old and New Testaments* (New York, Carlton, 1857)